Walking
Perth

PERTH

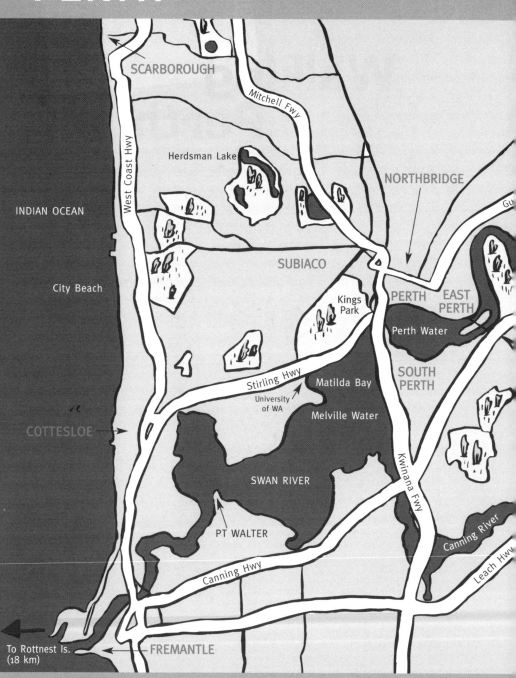

Walking
Perth

RON CRITTALL

NEW
HOLLAND

First published in Australia in 2000 by
New Holland Publishers (Australia) Pty Ltd
Sydney • Auckland • London • Cape Town

14 Aquatic Drive Frenchs Forest NSW 2086 Australia
218 Lake Road Northcote Auckland New Zealand
24 Nutford Place London W1H 6DQ United Kingdom
80 McKenzie Street Cape Town 8001 South Africa

National Library of Australia
Cataloguing-in-Publication Data:
  Crittall, Ron.
  Walking Perth.
  Bibliography.
  Includes index.
  ISBN 1 86436 451 3
  Walking – Western Australia – Perth – Guidebooks.
  2. Perth (W.A.) – Guidebooks. I. Title.
  919.4110466

Publishing Manager: Anouska Good
Project Editor: Jennifer Lane
Designer: Peta Nugent
Artwork: Mitch Vane
Maps: Priscilla Nielsen
Layout: Melbourne Media Services
Printer: Times Offset, Malaysia

Contents

Preface

My wife and I had been here for five years when we realised that Perth was where we would stay. It had been just another stop on our slow working perambulation around the world with no intention to settle. Now, after twenty-eight years here, we know it was the right—the best—decision. There were several factors. The climate—we liked being warm. The feel of a city of a manageable size, one that's not rushing at a million miles an hour. Where there's quiet, accessible beauty. And, most of all, the people. They have the time and the inclination to be friendly and helpful.

Writing the book has shown me how much I did not know about my adopted city. There are hidden little byways, tales of heartbreak and discovery, and gloriously secluded quiet places. Even some of the familiar places and things took on new meaning as I dug around.

My first thanks go to Barry Strickland, who involved me in his Guided City Walks several years ago, and showed me so much of old Perth. Thanks also to fellow author Liz Byrski, who introduced me to New Holland. My gratitude finally goes to those special friends who cheerfully became my guinea pigs—checking out the walks—especially Paddy Greenhalgh who has walked every one.

Then there were the many people in government departments, local council offices, libraries and historical societies who willingly gave me their time and knowledge. All this help just confirmed my opinion about Perth people and their friendliness. Last, but not least, Gary Bateman and his staff at Serco, who sorted out bus and train routes and times, to ensure that you don't get lost or stranded.

Ron Crittall

Introduction

Perth dominates the enormous, though empty state of Western Australia. Although the state is ten times the size of the United Kingdom, it is home to less than two million people. Seventy-five per cent of that population live in the capital, Perth. Originally hugging the banks of the Swan River, the city and its suburbs occupy a great chunk of largely flat coastal plain between the Darling Range and the Indian Ocean, and sprawl either side of the Swan River as it winds to the sea.

Although Perth borders the ocean, and gentle surf rolls up the long, clean white beaches, the river is the soul of Perth, not the sea. Upstream of the city centre, the Swan is just an ordinary waterway. Opposite and below the city it broadens out to form a wide expanse—a lake in all but name. Here it provides light, reflection, inspiration and a playground for young and old. Triangles of canvas and nylon, of all colours and sizes, speckle the broad sheltered waters which sparkle and glitter with the sea breeze. Downstream it narrows again, just before passing through Fremantle Harbour and into the Indian Ocean.

One of Perth's great attributes is that the sea and river frontages are public land and accessible to everyone. The grassy areas along the shoreline are full of families picnicking under tall gum trees. Fishermen waste time and bait along the river banks, while cyclists, joggers and dog owners make their way along the adjacent pathways, and kites fly high when the breeze strengthens. Pelicans and black swans idly paddle back and forth in secluded, reed-fringed bays, while, ever-present in the background, tall office towers glint in the afternoon sun.

A thousand mining and exploration companies are based here in Perth. The neon signs of these mineral giants and oil companies jostle for prominence with those of banks and insurance firms. They bring a touch of the brash frontier town, a feeling aided by the knowledge that Perth is the world's most isolated continental capital. Its nearest neighbour, Adelaide, is 2,700 kilometres away by road, while Singapore is 3,900 by air. But in spite of the shining glass, concrete and steel, Perth doesn't really see itself as a major international city.

Remnants of Perth's early British heritage are interspersed between new office blocks. There are several churches, the Town Hall, and a courthouse, while ornate hotels and theatres, and the Perth Mint date from the Gold Rush of a hundred years ago. The discovery of gold at Coolgardie and Kalgoorlie transformed both state and city and much the same has happened during the Mineral Boom of the last thirty-five years.

The City proper forms a narrow rectangle along four east–west streets, parallel to the river. St Georges Terrace is the main commercial street, and as such, is a canyon-like home to most of the highrise buildings. In contrast, broad, open parkland lies between river and city. Kings Park, at the western end of the rectangle, is Perth's jewel. One thousand acres of pristine natural bushland, it occupies a prime position above city and river. At the eastern end of the city is a monument of another kind—the Burswood Casino.

Getting around Perth is easy. There are good suburban bus and rail services, and while Perth is a city built for cars, pedestrians aren't forgotten either. The two main shopping blocks in the city are vehicle free, and linked by shopping arcades. More and more walkways are being built.

The café society is thriving in both city and suburbs. Now, cafés are not only places to be seen in, they're out in the open. Despite the Mediterranean climate, eating out of doors was banned for many years. These days tables and chairs shaded by coloured umbrellas, spread across pavements and any other available outdoor area—ready for coffee and conversation.

Perth has absorbed something of the outback outlook on life. There's a feeling of space, an independence of view and style, and it's retained some of that country friendliness. Visitors are welcomed and even taxi drivers are cheerful and efficient.

Walking Perth is a guide to many special places in and around the city. Some walks cover obvious areas, such as the centres of Perth and Fremantle, with their historic and modern buildings, parks, malls and people. Several take in the Swan River in its various widths and moods, three walks are in the natural bushland of the hills, and two walks are set aside for exploring the magical island of Rottnest. Some places buzz with activity and humanity, while others reveal a surprising availability of quiet, secluded nooks for peaceful contemplation.

Perth is a dynamic city. It's constantly changing—new parks, roads and developments—with corresponding disruption. I've tried to identify the main changes happening over the next two years, but invariably there will be walks where time and edict will have made directions inaccurate, for which I apologise and hope you don't get lost.

Many recent changes have been for the better. There has been a greater appreciation of heritage, and the need to add to what was already there, rather than replace it. Finally, there has been greater recognition of the humble walker, with the provision of more malls, walkways and easier access to places and facilities.

Walks in central Perth are listed first. Each walk has a short summary to give you some of the flavour and emphasis of that walk. The walks range in distance from 1.5 to 10 kilometres, though most are between 4 and 5 kilometres. An approximate time for each is given, based on my walking team's experience (and we didn't rush). The idea is to enjoy the walk and have time to look, consider and savour. Page 9 lists the walks in order of length.

Perth has very little steep terrain. The few walks with steep slopes or rough surfaces contain specific advice. As a general rule, take comfortable walking shoes, a hat, sunscreen and water. The main consideration for most walks is the weather. Perth has a Mediterranean type of climate, so the summers are hot and dry, and the winters are mild and (occasionally) wet. Hot weather mostly occurs between December and March. This means tempera-

tures which rise to over 35°C, but Perth's humidity is usually low—a blessing which makes the heat bearable.

The summer wind pattern is one of land and sea breezes, with the sea breeze, affectionately called the Fremantle Doctor, bringing cooling relief.

Summer walking is best in the mornings, and the earlier the better. Afternoons are only recommended if there's an early sea breeze. Most spring and autumn days bring balmy weather, ideal for walking at any hour, and there are many fine days between winter storms.

Weather forecasts in Perth are generally accurate. They can be found in the daily paper, or by phoning 1196.

All walks assume a starting point in central Perth, with transport information (where relevant) defined from there. There's a Free Transit Zone covering the central city. It's great, use it.

Public transport is most frequent on weekdays, especially during morning and evening rush hours. Saturday services are less frequent and some Sunday bus services only start at 10am and run at two hour intervals. It is a good idea to check bus times, especially for the more remote walks (phone: Transperth: 13 62 13).

Perth's suburban trains are fast, frequent, clean and comfortable. There are four lines that meet at Perth Central in the form of an 'X'. The Fremantle line crosses to become the Midland line, while Currambine links to the Armadale line. You must buy tickets from automatic machines before travelling. A broad network of bus routes covers the city and suburbs. Perth also has Central Area Transit (CAT) buses—low-slung grey vehicles—which traverse the central blocks frequently and without charge. The only public ferry service is across Perth Water, running between Barrack Square and South Perth. Ferries to Rottnest Island are run by private operators (see newspaper advertisements for details).

Perth's History

The land alongside the Swan River was, for thousands of years, the home of the local Aboriginal people who moved around the region hunting, fishing and gathering, according to the seasons. They made great use of the river banks, because access to food was easier here, and the river became particularly important in their culture. Their lives were to change dramatically with the arrival of the white settlers.

It was in 1829 that Captain James Stirling sailed out from England and selected the site for his new colony's capital. Stirling seems to have been determined to establish his Swan River Colony despite evidence that this was not a good spot for a predominantly agricultural settlement.

Earlier Dutch (Willem de Vlamingh 1697) and French (Nicolas Baudin 1801) expeditions had concluded that the Swan Valley had little appeal. Stirling made his first exploratory expedition here in 1827 and either did not look very hard at his surroundings, or chose to ignore what existed. His decision was the result of optimism succeeding over reality. He made Perth the site of his colony's capital for practical, aesthetic and strategic reasons. Immediately upstream, the Heirisson Islands marked the limit of navigation. As a naval officer, Stirling saw the towering limestone bluff of Mt Eliza (later incorporated into Kings Park), and the adjacent Narrows as providing a good point for defence— presumably against possible French intervention. It was also a beautiful location, and perhaps he envisaged the infant city enclosed within the twin charms of Perth Water and Kings Park.

The settlers at the time did not recognise the advantages that we can see today. The Swan Valley plain was (and is) sand, sand

and more sand, with occasional limestone ridges, and a few pockets of alluvial soil. When the settlers arrived in 1829, lured by visions of English type farming country, they were bitterly disappointed.

The appeal of the Swan River Colony soon evaporated and Stirling's settlement languished and stagnated. Many settlers stayed and made a go of things, but there was no labour market, so it was difficult to get anything major done.

This had been touted as a 'free' colony, but eventually convicts were seen as the only solution. The British Government was more than willing to co-operate, because New South Wales and Tasmania had recently stopped accepting them. The first boatload arrived in 1850, supposedly carrying a 'better class' of convict, and by 1868 almost ten thousand had been sent to Western Australia.

Because they were British convicts, their care was a British responsibility, and Pensioner Guards (mostly retired soldiers) came out as overseers. The guards were encouraged to settle here, so many came with their families. At much the same time, two thousand Irish serving girls were recruited – to correct the gender imbalance in the population.

The supply of convicts made an enormous difference. Public works could be carried out and numerous roads, bridges, jetties, courthouses and so on were built. These included some of Perth's finest heritage buildings, such as Government House, Perth Town Hall, Fremantle Gaol and Fremantle Arts Centre and Museum. Western Australia's population increased fourfold in under twenty years.

For the first fifty years, Perth's main transport artery was the Swan River. Roads were difficult to build and travel along due to the sandy surface. All this changed with the building of the railway from Fremantle to Perth and on to Guildford in 1881.

The next major event, and perhaps the most important of all, was the discovery of gold, first at Coolgardie in 1892 and then a year later at Kalgoorlie. This transformed both state and city almost beyond belief.

The resulting Gold Rush brought many thousands of fortune-seekers to Western Australia. Most came first to Perth, not knowing how far away Kalgoorlie really was. Tent cities were created to house the hopeful, new industries established, and services extended. The influx placed enormous demands on the government to upgrade roads and railways, schools and other public facilities. It also meant that suddenly there was money—money for public works, money for private ventures, and money for extravagance. Entrepreneurs, architects and engineers flooded into Western Australia and there was an exuberant explosion of hotels, theatres, banks and shops.

One of the biggest challenges facing the state, was providing Kalgoorlie with a reliable water supply. Enter C. Y. O'Connor, a brilliant engineer who designed and constructed the Goldfields Water Scheme, pumping water nearly 600 kilometres from

Mundaring just outside Perth. This was one of the great engineering feats of the time. O'Connor also created the Fremantle Harbour that we now have.

O'Connor and Western Australia were fortunate in having Sir (later Lord) John Forrest in power at the time. He was Premier in this critical period for Western Australia, and led the state into the Australian Federation in 1901. It was at this time that Western Australia became involved in its first overseas conflict, the Boer War in South Africa. That was merely the overture to the First World War which had such a devastating effect upon the entire country, but paradoxically created a nation. The loss of so much manpower brought development and growth in Perth, as elsewhere, to a standstill.

Between the wars there were land settlement schemes to help ex-servicemen, and the first of the 20th century migration schemes, initially for British citizens wanting to come to Australia. The transcontinental railway and the first airlines began the task of physically bringing the far-flung parts of Australia together—after the Anzacs had created the emotional ties.

The Second World War once more took many Perth residents away to a war, one that was closer to home with the involvement of Japan. Gun positions were set up in Fremantle and Rottnest, and American influence arrived. The years after this war saw floods of migrants, not just from the United Kingdom but also refugees from the war-devastated states of Europe. From 1945 onwards, the population of Perth grew by over 100,000 per decade and its multicultural society was born.

The minerals boom, which began in the 1960s, was based on the exploitation of enormous deposits of iron ore, bauxite and nickel, and had a similar effect to the Gold Rush. Remote areas of the state were opened up, and once again Perth was affected dramatically. A new construction boom saw the face of Perth change almost beyond recognition. St Georges Terrace, which had been a repository of glorious buildings of individual style and character, was transformed into a canyon of high-rises. Throughout the city the verandah posts and balconies which had adorned many older buildings sadly disappeared because of the danger to pedestrians, should their supporting posts be knocked down by vehicles. Suddenly much of the city was naked.

New (concrete) clothes appeared in the form of the Narrows Bridge and its freeways, but with the associated loss of Mounts Bay, the Pensioner Barracks, and the unimpeded view to Mt Eliza.

In the sixties Australia again went to war, this time in Vietnam. This, combined with growing economic ties, turned the focus much more to Asia. More refugees, especially from Vietnam, increased Perth's multicultural mix which is perhaps most obvious in the range of restaurants that now exist. Northbridge was revitalised by this change, and by recognition of the Cultural Precinct.

Constant growth in population saw suburbs spread ever further away from the city centre, resulting in the coronation of the car as 'king'. Perth has one of the highest ratios of cars to population of any place on earth.

In the early 1980s, a group of West Australians led by Alan Bond, won yachting's 'Holy Grail', the America's Cup. This meant that the defence of the trophy was held in the waters off Fremantle in 1987, and the lead up to this event gave that city a much-needed facelift. Its Victorian and Edwardian streetscapes were revamped and restored, creating a superb environment which is still attracting the crowds. Western Australia's entrepreneurs and their paper empires crashed in 1987 – as did the State Government. It had been involved in secret deals with these operators, in what became known as 'WA Inc'. The State Premier, and others, ended up in prison.

The last decade has seen a different approach, and different priorities. It's no longer development at any price, and the value of retaining the past has been recognised. Pedestrians are finally being given space and safety. Walkways extend along both sides of the Swan River, along the Indian Ocean coastline, and through various heritage areas. The city centre has two pedestrian malls, the heritage precinct will soon become accessible and the river foreshore is being brought back into the city, rather than being cut off by whizzing traffic.

There is hope indeed, far more than James Stirling and his despondent settlers could have dreamed of in 1829.

Key to Maps

 Hospital

 Church

 Parks and gardens

 Information

 Parking

 Bus stop

 Post office

 Gallery

 Public toilets

 Railway station

Route Marks

••▶••• route of walk

7 key numbers

S walk start

F walk finish

An easy-to-follow illustrative map accompanies each walk. The walk route is clearly marked in green; buildings and sites are dark blue; parks and gardens are green; and 'general' areas are shaded light blue.

On each map the walk route begins at the point **S** and finishes at **F**. Key numbers are located on the map as well as in the walk text. The Key to Maps, left, displays full details of symbols that appear on the maps in order to assist the walker.

Walks in Order of Length

Heritage Precinct | 1.5 km
City East | 2.3 km
City Central | 2.5 km
City West | 2.8 km
University of WA | 3 km
Fremantle | 3.5 km
Convicts to Cappuccinos | 4 km
Herdsman Lake | 4 km
Northbridge | 4 km
Rottnest Walk Two | 4 km
Springtime at Araluen | 4 km
West Perth | 4 km
East Perth | 4.4 km
Cottesloe | 4.5 km
South Perth | 4.6 km
Guildford | 5 km
Kings Park | 5 km
Rottnest Walk One | 5 km
Subiaco | 5 km
Burswood | 5.3 km
Mundaring Weir | 6 km
Point Walter | 6.5 km
Perth Water | 7 km
Mounts & Matilda Bays | 8 km
John Forrest Heritage Walk | 10.2 km

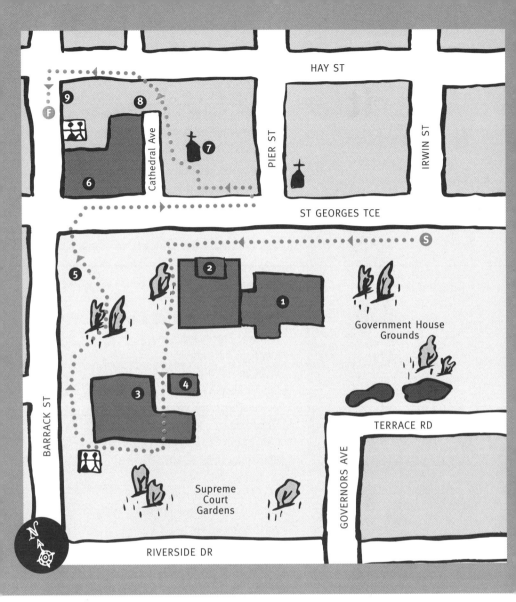

HAY ST

PIER ST

IRWIN ST

Cathedral Ave

F

9

8

7

6

St GEORGES TCE

S

5

2

1

Government House Grounds

3

4

BARRACK ST

TERRACE RD

GOVERNORS AVE

Supreme Court Gardens

RIVERSIDE DR

N

Walk key

1. Government House | 2. Council House | 3. The Supreme Court | 4. Old Courthouse |
5. Stirling Gardens | 6. Central Government Building | 7. St Georges Anglican Cathedral |
8. Land Titles Office | 9. Perth Town Hall

Heritage Precinct

Government and Church—where Perth began...

Start

Vehicle entrance to Government House, opposite the corner of St Georges Terrace and Irwin Street. A short walk from the city centre or take any bus along St Georges Terrace to the Victoria Ave/Concert Hall stop.

Finish

Perth Town Hall, corner Barrack and Hay streets.

Length/Time

1.5 km/1.5 hours

Wheelchairs

Diversions needed from Old Courthouse to Barrack Street and to main entrance of St Georges Cathedral via Cathedral Avenue.

Within a few weeks of Captain James Stirling and the first settlers landing in 1829, Perth was laid out on a low sandy ridge parallel to the Swan River. Tents were erected on what is now Stirling Square, the military barracks were built on what became Barrack Street, and the Church and other official buildings soon followed. The first Government House ('hut' would be more accurate) was here, and the first Anglican church (the Rush Church) was built nearby. Hefty chunks of land were set aside for government purposes, and much is still dedicated to those uses.

This walk explores this area, and the numerous buildings of the Colonial era which still exist.

Government House |1| is situated in three hectares of gardens, with extensive lawns, superb rose gardens, and several 'Royal' trees, planted by successive royal visitors. The small plaque on the gatepost commemorates an earlier Government House sited just inside the boundary. It was built between 1835 and 1838, but suffered greatly from leaks and white ants, creating a need for the current building.

Setting out westward along St Georges Terrace towards the city centre you will pass several of the 1979 sesquicentenary plaques set into the pavement. The second one, for the year 1833, is named after Yagan who, at the time of settlement, was leader of the local Aboriginal people. He was killed following a series of altercations with colonists. The church across the road, built in 1906, is St Andrews, originally Presbyterian but now Uniting Church.

Much of Government House and its gardens can be seen from the pavement. Just to the left of the tennis court is an ancient, gnarled olive tree, supposedly planted in the 1830s.

The House itself, one of the most attractive of Perth's old buildings, is built of local bricks and limestone. Constructed between 1859 and 1863, using convict labour, the opening was sufficiently grand to be recorded in the *London Illustrated News*. The style of architecture is best defined as Tudor Gothic, and the turrets echo those of the Tower of London.

Anthony Trollope wrote in 1873: '*Perth I found to be a very pretty town, built on a lake of brackish water formed by the Swan River. It contains 6000 inhabitants, and of course is the residence of the chief people of the colony. The governor's house is handsome, as is also the town hall. The churches—cathedrals I should call them—both of the Protestants and Roman Catholics, are large and convenient.*'

Continue to the end of the gardens, where a driveway goes past a tall T-jointed building which is Council House. Down the drive you can see the red-tiled brick and limestone Government House Ballroom, designed in 1899 by John Grainger (father of musician and songwriter Percy).

Council House |2|, the home of the Perth City Council, replaced a hodgepodge of old Government buildings in 1961. Its design was the result of a national competition. The winning entry made this one of the first buildings in Perth to have air conditioning, and to use the principles of solar design. It was completed just in time for the Commonwealth Games that were held in Perth in 1962. Go into Council House. The spacious ground floor lobby has occasional art exhibitions, but otherwise there are displays of memorabilia and gifts to the Perth City Council—and a multimedia information kiosk. In the mid-1990s it was the centre of controversy when it was found to contain asbestos. Despite strong moves for its demolition, the council opted to refurbish it. That job has been completed and the building looks spanking new, though it's still out of character and proportion with the rest of the precinct. Return to the Terrace and turn left until you come face to face with three brass kangaroos alongside a curving pool of water. These are the work of Charles and Joan Smith, the same sculptors who created the Burswood Heritage Trail (see Walk 10). The 'Mob of Kangaroos' has been designed to 'bound through the urban space of the site, in full flight, creating an awesome, inspiring vision'.

Turn back a few paces, and enter the gardens next to the 'Giant Stone Shish Kebab'. This unusual monument, *The Ore Obelisk*, displaying different ores, cele- brates the impact of the 1960s mineral boom upon the state, and WA reaching a population of one million. It was revamped in 1997, and diamond-bearing rock added. The details are recorded in two sets of inscriptions (that are difficult to read) at the bottom of the pole.

The Supreme Court |3| is situated further down the pathway that runs alongside Council House. It was also designed by John Grainger, and completed in 1903. It is worth going into the entrance hall to see the imposing staircase leading to the upper balconies, and the three coloured glass domes. You will also find displays of old maps and photos, a drinking fountain, self-service vending machines, and toilets.

On coming out of the Supreme Court, there's a simple inconspicuous single-storey structure, half hidden over to the right. A plain, squat porch marks the entrance to Perth's oldest building, the **Old Courthouse** |4|, dating from 1837.

Opening Times

Government House Gardens: Tues 12 noon–2pm.
The Supreme Court: weekdays 10am–4pm.
Francis Burt Law Education Centre and Museum (the Old Courthouse): Mon–Fri, 10am–2pm.
St Georges Cathedral: daily from 7am–5pm.

Refreshments

Cafés near the end of the walk, and vending machines in the Supreme Court.

The colony was so new and so poor that it also served as a schoolroom when court wasn't sitting (this was the first Government boys' school in Australia), as church on Sundays, and as a concert hall. Dom Salvado, a Benedictine monk, walked 130 kilometres back to Perth in 1846 to raise money for his newly established Aboriginal mission at New Norcia. A concert pianist of note, he performed here with assistance from the Catholic, Anglican, Methodist and Jewish communities.

The Old Courthouse is now the Francis Burt Law Education Centre and Museum and is well worth a visit. The interior is surprisingly spacious. The jarrah floorboards and open timber roof are largely original, though the furniture is not.

Walk back past the Law Library (next door), and down the steep steps to the left. Proceed along the alley and through the small car park on the right. This was river 100 years ago. The elegant rear arched balconies of the Supreme Court (more attractive than the front) used to look out over the Swan River, before reclamation created what are now the Supreme Court Gardens on the left.

Follow the driveway up the slope toward the double gates. This is approximately where Stirling first landed in 1829, and the park to your right is the **Stirling Gardens |5|**. Take the path to the right, between the gates and the large clump of bamboo. Just across the road is the balconied Weld (gentlemen's) Club with its attractive bell tower. In the 19th century this was one of

Perth Town Hall.

the main spheres of influence in the colony. Follow the path to the paved area surrounded by towering trees in the middle of the garden. Stirling Gardens was established as a botanical garden in the first days of the colony, and declared a public park in 1845. Some of the trees are well over one hundred years old. Benches and deckchairs are available for quiet contemplation.

Turn half left towards the major traffic intersection, passing a memorial to victims of the Holocaust, and through the Stirling Gardens gates. The statue is that of Alexander Forrest. In the late 19th century, both as explorers and politicians, Alexander and his brother John (who became Premier of Western Australia) had an enormous impact upon the state. Alexander helped open up the vast Kimberley region, and became Mayor of Perth.

Directly across the Terrace is the Treasury, or **Central Government Building |6|**.Western Australia had three successive Colonial Architects (Richard Jewell, George Temple Poole and John Grainger) who made major contributions to the city, and all were involved in either the original design of this building or its subsequent additions. If you look carefully you can detect varied brick-work from the different periods. They're all laid in the Flemish Bond pattern, where coloured bricks are laid alternately length-wise and end on.

Cross over the Terrace (with the lights) to the Treasury Buildings. Turn right across the front, and at the end you will find two small plaques which mark the spot from where all Perth distances are measured. Part of the building was the GPO for many years, and the 'zero' definition stayed when the Post Office moved.

This corner, at Cathedral Avenue, provides the best vantage point for view-ing **St Georges Anglican Cathedral |7|**, a fairly simple brick building with limestone adornments, and at the back, a square bell tower. The bells ring on Tuesday evenings from 6pm–8pm, and on Sundays from 9am–10am and 4pm–5pm.

The cathedral was the third church erected on this site. The first was a tempo-rary Rush Church (the walls were made with rushes), used as church and court until the Old Courthouse was constructed. Then, in 1845 St Georges Church was opened to the left of where the Cathedral is, with a 'contemptible pepperpot' tower.

It wasn't considered appropriate for a cathedral so the current building was then erected between 1880 and 1888. Continue along the Terrace, past the Cathedral Shop, to the Deanery, dating from 1859. It is thought the design (looking like a doll's house) came from a pattern book, rather like dresses do today. The photograph outside shows the old pepperpot Church in the background.

Retrace your steps to go up the stairs next to the Cathedral Shop, above which is the Burt Memorial Hall. Note the cross on the pillar at the top of the stairs. This was removed from Westminster Abbey during restoration work, and donated to Perth. Turn left here and go around to the main entrance of the Cathedral. Inside, it takes on a totally different scale and feeling. The vaulted brick arches and soaring jarrah ceil-ings create a surprisingly spacious and appealing place of worship. The jarrah beams were soaked in the Swan River before use, to make them more malleable.

It is worth exploring the cathedral and volunteer guides are usually available between 9am–3pm. There are memorials to colonial pioneers and Great War victims, a wrought iron chancel screen, and the Soldiers' Memorial Chapel, which is on the left hand side. This features a graveside cross from the Flanders battlefields, and a Victoria Cross. The chapel also gives a fine view of the main altar and the superb alabaster reredos behind it.

As you leave the Cathedral the last additions to the Treasury are directly ahead of you. Go up the ramp to the right, and stop by the end of the sunken driveway. The building to the left is the **Land Titles Office** |8|, finished in 1897.

Designed by Poole, it has been described as the finest Free Classical building in Australia. The extravagant exterior reflects the funds available after the discovery of gold. Note the contrast with the simplicity and relative lack of decorative features in the earlier buildings.

Unfortunately, structural problems have necessitated the erection of fencing and scaffolding to protect passers by. This necessity has been turned into a virtue (creating public art) by building a copper 'replication' of the hidden facade. Both this and the Treasury Buildings are in limbo while the Government seeks expressions of interest from the private sector, for refurbishment and some future use.

The Law Chambers, to the right, has been allowed to protrude into this heritage area and interrupts the view of, and approach to, the Land Titles Office. An ugly building, it has prompted numerous suggestions that it be dismantled and removed so that this precinct can be recreated as it once was. The excellent Perth City Library is in the basement.

Follow the narrow passage in front of the Land Titles Office, through to Hay Street. Note the reflections in the glass facade of Cinema City (opposite), and cross over this one way street. You now have a view of the end of the Land Titles Office, and to the right, of the **Perth Town Hall** |9|. This was built with convict labour between 1867 and 1870 to a clean and uncluttered design by Jewell. The recently cleaned exterior shows its coloured bricks and Flemish Bond pattern to best advantage. Its clock tower has some unusual features.

The hall itself, with a superb jarrah floor and ceiling, is upstairs. Originally there was an arched undercroft for a market, which was not a success. Later, it became the first home of the Perth Volunteer Fire Brigade. When the alarm went, local taxi drivers would get rid of their clients, drive to the Town Hall and unhitch their horses so they could pull the fire wagons.

The mismatched granite facing was installed in 1957, three years before another disaster. The buildings on either side of the Town Hall were the 19th century Guardhouse and Legislative Council.

These were pulled down to make way for an appalling bank structure. The Government of the 1990s redressed this by demolishing the bank, but the future of the land (hidden behind hoardings) is tied up with the privatisation of the other nearby Government offices.

Go to the intersection of Hay and Barrack streets, so called because the original army barracks were nearby. Cross to the foot of the clock tower, which features a memorial to HMAS *Perth*. A few steps down Barrack Street brings you to some public toilets and the apologetic shuttered staircase that leads up to the Town Hall itself. Over the next few years the building is to be restored to its original state, and the hall made more accessible.

Just beyond, where the hoarding starts again, is the spot where, on 12 August 1829, Mrs Helen Dance, wife of the commander of HMS *Sulphur*, chopped down a tree (she may have swung the axe once, but it was really felled by sailors), to christen the new Town of Perth. There is a statue and plaque to commemorate this, but they are in storage awaiting the redevelopment. The walk finishes here, in the place where Perth began.

Walk key

1. Perth Railway Station |
2. Forrest Place |
3. Murray Street Mall |
4. Hay Street Mall |
5. London Court | 6. Atlas Building | 7. Palace Hotel |
8. Trinity Church |
9. Wesley Church |
10. Horseshoe Bridge

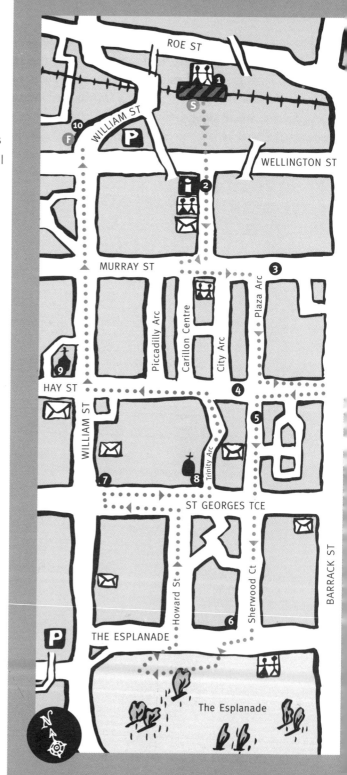

City Central
The heart of the city

Start
The main ground floor entrance of the Perth Railway Station, in Wellington Street.

Finish
Horseshoe Bridge, between the Railway Station and the bus station.

Length/Time
2.5 km/2 hours

Wheelchairs
Access to some buildings is not possible. Divert from Atlas Building to Howard Street, and take the Trinity Arcade lift to Hay Street level.

In the original plans for Perth, it was envisaged that St Georges Terrace would be the most important address, and that 'No. 2' street would be Hay Street. It has been that way ever since. The grand commercial buildings are in the terrace, while Hay and Murray Streets became retail-orientated.

Wellington Street was a backwater, literally so, until a string of lakes which covered that side of Perth were drained and the railway line built on the reclaimed land.

The long city blocks were a hindrance to north–south movement, so a series of arcades were built between the main streets, and these still exist.

Ever since the railway from Freman-tle to Guildford was built, it has been a social and physical barrier splitting the city in two. Numerous plans to move, sink, or build over the tracks have so far come to nought. One day something might happen. **Perth Railway Station |1|** is a pleasant, standard 19th century building. Directly in front is a pedestrian crossing over Welling-ton Street, and on either side and in front are ugly pedestrian bridges ('featuring' green cross-members) which effectively conceal everything beyond them.

Walk over the road, up the steps, and under the pedestrian bridge. Immediately on your right is the Western Australia Tourist Office, with much useful information about Perth and Western Australia. **Forrest Place |2|** opens in front of you. Named after Lord John Forrest (one of the founders of Federation, and the first Australian-born peer) this is the first part of the city to owe its development to the Federal Govern-ment, which acquired the land in 1911 (Federation occurred in 1901). The striking General Post Office was built between 1914 and 1923, and the complementary Commonwealth Bank in the 1930s. Forrest Place is the city's main plaza, used for vari-ous public events. It also used to be the public forum, until a political meeting in 1974 got a bit rough.

Forrest Chase, to the left, is a major shop-ping complex, home to Myers department store. This was the site of Boan Brothers which was Western Australia's biggest store until bought out and demolished by Myers.

The GPO's main hall lacks character and is rather sad, being no longer in use. The Commonwealth Bank's main chamber is much better, partly because it is still used. The Forrest Place entrance has been closed, so enter around the corner in Murray Street. Note the quotations under the clocks at either end of the chamber.

Murray Street Mall |3| is full of flower and fruit stalls, buskers, charity stands, cafés and drinking fountains. Several arcades (Piccadilly in front of you; Plaza, City and Carillon to the left) go through to Hay Street. Take the Plaza Arcade, and part way along you will come to the Transperth Information Centre, with details on all the metropolitan transport services.

The **Hay Street Mall |4|** has a much more attractive and historic streetscape than Murray. Look at the fading charms of the upper levels of the building to the left of London Court. This was the Theatre Royal, Perth's first real post Gold Rush entertain-ment venue. Behind the splendid decora-tive plaster work, part of the theatre's shell is still home to a Hoyts cinema.

Opposite is another relic, the Savoy Hotel, with its grand wedding cake bal-conies, while high above is a flying statue: of Percy Button, tightrope walker. This is one of several pieces of public art placed here in the mall to entertain and intrigue.

Go left along the mall and past Aherns, Perth's largest home-grown department store. On the right hand corner, opposite the clock tower of Perth Town Hall (see Walk No. 1), is the McNess Royal Arcade, which was one of the first ornate Gold Rush buildings. On the other corner is a Perth institution, T. Sharp and Company, tobacconists here for one hundred years—but they can only call themselves 'Pen Specialists' now!

Return along Hay Street and turn into London Court |5|. This lovely narrow arcade built in mock Tudor style was modelled on Liberty's store in London, and leads through to St Georges Terrace. The clocks at either end have tableaux that perform every quarter hour.

St Georges Terrace is a street of lost grandeur and lost opportunities. Full of superb individual buildings in the 1930s, they're almost all gone, replaced by faceless high rises. Directly opposite is one of the few innovative and attractive skyscrapers, the aluminium-clad Allendale Square, set imaginatively at 45 degrees to the street.

Take the pedestrian crossing over the Terrace and go down the adjacent one-way street, Sherwood Court, past the enormous blue glass Exchange Plaza. The last building on the left, Lawson Apartments (1930s art deco), was for many years one of the few residential developments in the city centre. It houses the Karrakatta Club, Perth's premier women's club.

Cross over Sherwood Court to the **Atlas Building |6|**, with its neoclassical brass and pink stone exterior. The main door and foyer have splendid art deco work, with much use of brass. It is worthwhile going inside and calling the lift. Pull open the two sliding doors to see the original gleaming brass-panelled interior.

Opening Times

Western Australia Tourist Office:
Mon–Thurs 8.30am–6pm;
Fri 8.30am–7pm; Sat 8.30am–5pm;
Sun 10am–5pm.
**Transperth Information Centre
(Plaza Arcade):** Mon–Thurs
8am–5.30pm; Fri 8am–7pm;
Sat 8am–5pm;
Sun 12 noon–5pm.
Esplanade Conservatory: Mon–Sat
10am–4pm; Sun 12 noon–4pm.
Palace Hotel (now Bankwest):
Mon–Fri 9.30am–4pm.
Wesley Church: Mon–Fri
9am–4pm.

Refreshments

Numerous cafés, hotels, restaurants and fast food outlets along the route.

The Atlas Building opens out on to The Esplanade, so named because this was the original river shoreline. The park and roads you see here today are all built on reclaimed land. Cross over through the Alf Curlewis Gardens entrance and turn right across the grass to the eye-catching glass pyramid, which is the Allan Green Conservatory. Look right to appreciate the striking contrast between the flat parkland and the canyon wall of skyscrapers.

Go along the brick path back to The Esplanade, where you will face Howard Street. The glass building on the right hand corner, with its unfriendly ground floor hoarding, took the place of one of Perth's jewels: the Esplanade Hotel, famous for Dame Nellie Melba singing from its balconies, and for creating the Pavlova dessert.

Cross The Esplanade and walk up Howard Street. Two thirds of the way up is a delightful turn of the century streetscape, on either side of the road. Continue up to St Georges Terrace, and note **Trinity Church |8|** across the road. Its unusual style has been called 'dissenter's medievalism'. Note too, the garish cross above the entrance. The original fell down in the 1968 earthquake and was only replaced twenty years later.

Turn left along St Georges Terrace, and walk to No. 101; originally the ES&A Bank in 1904, now the Western Australian Club, it is one of the few untouched Terrace relics.

The best known relic is across the road. After the senseless destruction of the Esplanade Hotel, preservation groups formed the 'Palace Guards' to defend this, the old **Palace Hotel |7|**. A developer, one Alan Bond, negotiated the erection of a high-rise behind the Palace in return for its preservation. The Bond Tower went up but the Palace never went back to being a hotel. Both are now part of Bankwest. It's still worth having a look at the interior following its refurbishment, even if it's now a banking chamber.

Cross the Terrace and go in through the main hotel entrance. The seemingly garish

The old Palace Hotel, now a Banking Chamber.

colours were based on detailed research which showed that this was the original appearance. The parquetry floor and the magnificent staircase climbing up the open foyer are superb. Continue past the statue and through the double doors into the old dining room, and imagine dining here in its heyday. The mirrors, the fans, and that ceiling! Return to the foyer and take the wood panelled lift (possibly the first in Perth) to the second floor. Walk down the first flight of stairs and through the museum door. The displays, beneath the massive steel and glass roof of modern architecture, give small intimations of past glories. Take the stairs back to the lobby, noting all the different decorative features. You can often see into one of the old rooms, full of moulded ceilings, tiled fireplaces, leather furniture, period paintings and thick carpets.

Back on St Georges Terrace, turn left towards **Trinity Church |8|**. Sesquicentennial (150 years since settlement) pavement plaques commemorate athletes Shirley Strickland and Herb Elliott, entertainer Rolf Harris, and two past Premiers of Western Australia: David Brand and Charles Court. Turn left into the arcade immediately past the church, go up the ramp and into the church. It is remarkably quiet and still, with an attractive balconied gallery. Continue up the ramp to the building with the traditional Flemish Bond brickwork, which is Church Hall No. 1, built in 1872. Immediately behind is Hall No. 2, which was the original Trinity Church of 1865. It is now the Trinity Lunch Room, 'a tradition since 1910', and still has its original vaulted timber ceiling.

Follow Trinity Arcade along its elegantly arched passageway, past its brass, glass and marble shopfronts, and back to the Hay Street Mall. Turn left into the mall. On the right are the bells of the Carillon Arcade; on the left, just before the end, is the skyscraper in miniature of Devon House, and next to it, Gledden Building, with its echoes of 1930s New York.

Diagonally across William Street is the **Wesley Church |9|**, built in 1867. The different coloured brickwork shows that the towers were added later, while the spire was damaged in the 1968 earthquake (and later repaired). The interior is quiet, restful and spacious—and surprisingly ornate for a Methodist church. Note the iron and timber gallery and the high jarrah ceiling. An unusual stained glass window, on the right hand side just beyond the gallery, shows an Aboriginal group with an Aboriginal Christ above them.

William is one of the ex-Royal streets. It was originally King William, after the English monarch, but the prefix got lost. St Georges Terrace was named King George's in 1829, but he died a year later, and somehow the saint took over.

Turn left along William Street to the next intersection, with Murray Street. Directly opposite is the 1928 Wentworth Hotel. Continue along William Street, past the entrance to Raine Square, and over the next intersection (Wellington Street). Look back to the corner you've just come from, at another ornate hotel, the Royal, surprisingly pre-Gold Rush. It has strong French influences, with the steep iron mansard roofs.

You are at the entrance to the **Horseshoe Bridge |10|** with cast iron black swans around the lampposts. It was built in 1903, in this shape in order to cross the railway line without embankments obstructing the roads on either side.

This is the end of the walk. The bus station is straight ahead, and the railway station main entrance is to the right along Wellington Street.

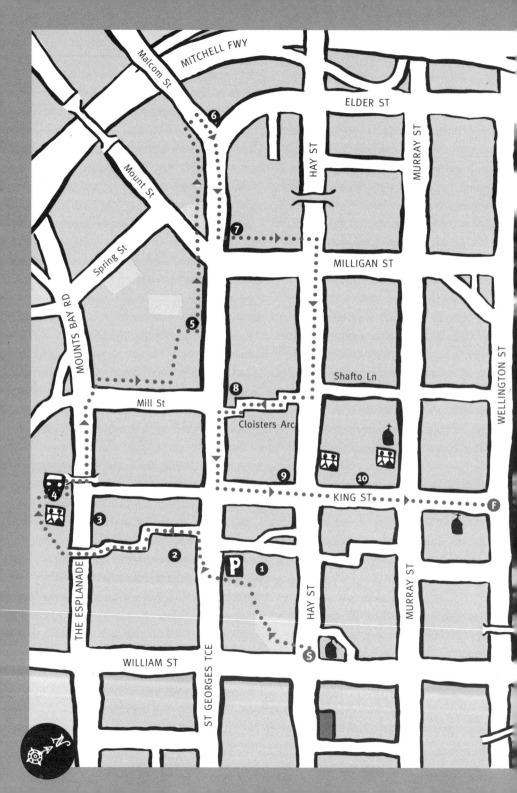

City West

The West End–a late developer with some forgotten corners

Start

Corner Hay and William streets, outside the Wesley Church.

Finish

Corner Wellington and King streets. Opposite bus station.

Length/Time

2.8 km/2.5–3 hours

Wheelchairs

Several sets of steps make this walk impractical for wheelchairs.

Walk key

1. Central Park Towers | 2. Perth Boys' School | 3. Westralia Square | 4. Busport | 5. St Georges Square | 6. Barracks Arch | 7. QV1 Building | 8. Cloisters | 9. His Majesty's Theatre | 10. King Street

The city, west of William Street, has always been quieter than the central blocks. More open, less hurried, fewer high rises.

That was until the Minerals Boom, when mining giants moved in, followed by insurance companies and government departments. The growth has occurred in pockets, leaving whole areas of two and three storey streetscapes untouched. Some have been refurbished into trendy enclaves, such as King Street, while others await the bulldozer or a sympathetic developer.

Some of the towers have stunning foyers, while the heavy hand of Government can be seen in the freeway system carving through this end of town, and in the 'white elephant' of the Perth Busport. In between, a few 19th century treasures still survive.

Cross Hay Street from Wesley Church and take the tree lined diagonal path through the small open park towards **Central Park Towers |1|**. This building, with tubular steel adornments, is Perth's tallest, at 290 metres. Cut past the rear of the Commonwealth Bank building and into the marble-lined foyer of Central Park. Unfortunately there's no access to the upper floors for sightseeing, but the abstract art installation across the back of the foyer is well worth looking at. Artist, Brian McKay, based his design on classical Greek architecture and used the same materials as in the building. The Cyrillic script, derived from a Greek church, illustrates 'cross cultural irony' by putting 13th century Byzantine into a '21st century' building.

Leave the foyer by the door next to the Cyrillic mural, moving out to St Georges Terrace (mind the steps). Across the road are three stone 1930s buildings—Newspaper House, and the Royal Insurance and Western Australia Trustee buildings. To the right is the red brick of Perth Technical College with its imposing little tower, built in 1910. These four buildings have been empty since the bottom dropped out of the property market in the late 1980s. They were part of the massive Westralia Square (rising behind the Tech) development, which has been in limbo since that time.

Cross St Georges Terrace and turn right. You will see some sesquicentenary pavement plaques, including one at the crossing to commemorate Richard Jewell, one of the great colonial architects, some of whose work can still be seen in Perth. The limestone building that looks like a church (it even has a cross over the entrance) was in fact the **Perth Boys' School |2|**. The Colonial Secretary who designed it was of the opinion that a godly structure inspired godly thoughts. The school, opened in 1852, was built from Rocky Bay (further down the Swan River) limestone, and you can see striations from the hand tools used to quarry the stone. The original broad floorboards, wooden shingle roof, and patch of wall with old names scrawled on it, are still visible inside, as well as the narrow church-like windows. Trying to study in the mid-summer heat, without ventilation, must have been appalling. The building, for years the National Trust Gift Shop, is now a café, called Reveleys after the original landowner, who actually built a water-powered flour mill there.

On leaving the school, turn left then walk along the raised footway immediately past Reveleys, and go through the archway labelled **Westralia Square |3|**, which is the large glass fronted building straight in front of you—the one completed part of the grand development. Behind the school, and the other empty buildings just visited, is an enormous hole. This excavation was for the main (unbuilt) part of the Westralia Square development. The natural slope of the land here was quite steep, and explains the presence of Reveley's Mill. Water came from the original Lake Kingsford (near the present Wellington Street), the slope generating the necessary power.

Continue down the footway, and turn left past the entrance of the Westralia Square building. Take the steps or elevator down to the first floor level, and proceed along the crossway over Mounts Bay Road to the **Busport |4|**. This was one of those bright ideas that did not work in practice. It was intended to encourage commuters to catch buses here rather than in the city centre.

The bus terminus is actually downstairs. Your level has three crossways, a series of shops and cafés, public toilets, and two roof garden areas. Go straight ahead through the shopping mall, passing on the right, the Transperth Information Centre which has full details on all the city's bus, train and ferry services.

The Winter Garden is to the left of the balcony at the end, and the Summer Garden to the right, though it is difficult to distinguish between them. The gardens are a pleasant spot to have a break, but views to the river and Kings Park are obstructed by the freeway. Go through the Summer Garden to the far end then turn towards, and cross Mounts Bay Road, following the signs to Mill Street. Take the steps down to street level, and turn right to cross Mill Street at the traffic lights. Turn right again to walk up Mill Street, a short, moderately steep road which got its name from another early flour mill. The Swan River Colony was meant to be an agricultural settlement, so the early settlers assumed that they would be able to grow, and process, wheat. It was a bitter lesson to find that the coastal plains were almost entirely sand.

Opening Times

Most commercial buildings open only during working hours. Friends of His Majesty's Theatre provide information and ad hoc tours: Mon–Fri 10am–4pm. Theatre tours Thurs 10.30am (a charge applies).

Refreshments

Numerous cafés, fast food outlets, and water fountains on the route.

On the other side of Mill Street is the Parmelia Hilton, one of Perth's five-star hotels. Go up the steps of No. 5 Mill Street, and around the right of the building, up the stairs and into the covered forecourt of Forrest Centre. The balconied brick building in front of you is Rigby's Bistro and Bar. Paul Rigby was one of Australia's top cartoonists, and there are copies of some of his cartoons in the bar. The building is a reproduction of the house occupied by Alexander Forrest (explorer and Lord Mayor) in the late 19th century.

Go round to the right of Rigby's, through the glass doors into **St Georges Square** |5|, and continue into the formal garden, laid out with several fountains and statues. Turn left at the central pond, which leads to a small area overlooking Bishop's House. This was built for the first Anglican Bishop, Mathew Hale, in 1859 in Georgian style, though the verandahs were added later. Note the Flemish Bond brickwork, the false windows by the chimney, and the horses' heads hitching posts next to the driveway.

Return up the centre of the garden and enter the rear of the office block, St Georges Square, built by an enlightened property developer, Lord McAlpine, British Tory and great fan of Western Australia's Broome. He created several highrises at this end of town, all with a touch of flair. The two foyers of this building are amongst the finest in Perth. They house the Wyllie Collection of Western Australian Landscape Art, from the 1830s on, with pieces from the state's most renowned artists. In the

Barracks Arch at the top of St Georges Terrace.

front foyer there is a picture of Mounts Bay as it was before reclamation of the river, and two sets of sketches by Henry Prinseps from the 1870s. The floral displays, the Aboriginal motif carpets, and the timber panelling (especially the front entrance) are splendid.

Go out into St Georges Terrace and turn left, noting the pavement plaque to Paddy Hannan, who discovered gold at Kalgoorlie and so helped transform the state and the city. Nos. 235–239 St Georges Terrace were dilapidated and due for demolition when McAlpine decided they were worthy of preservation—and matched thoughts with actions. Cross Mount Street with the lights and pass the briefcase-carrying kangaroos.

This sculpture *Going Home* is one of the pieces of public art erected by the City Council as part of its 'Perth, a City for the People' campaign. The Florence Hummerston Reserve on the left is a tiny oasis filled with tall trees, calling birds and the McNess Memorial.

Continue up the hill, and at the top of St Georges Terrace is the lonely brick **Barracks Arch |6|**. This is all that is left of the Pensioner Guard Barracks, demolished to make way for the freeway. Beyond is Parliament House (Walk 6), and you can appreciate the original plan for it to look down the full length of the Terrace. In 1966, then Premier David Brand wanted the Arch removed but, following public outcry, he agreed to an open vote in Parliament. His proposal was defeated, the Arch stayed, and Parliament House does not have an uninterrupted view.

Cross, with the lights, over to the Arch, with its explanatory plaques. It's easy, and sad, to imagine the two wings of the Barracks stretching away to left and right. Richard Jewell is thought to have had some involvement in the design, and there is the typical Flemish Bond brickwork. This is where the bricks have been laid alternately lengthwise and end on, usually with different coloured bricks, to create an interesting pattern. Note the pavement plaque to C. Y. O'Connor who worked here and designed the great Goldfields Water Scheme (see Walk 24) and Fremantle Harbour (see Walk 17). There are good views of Parliament House, of the city down St Georges Terrace, and of the First Church of Christ Scientist (it's not a mausoleum) to the left.

Face the city centre and head down the left side of the Terrace, past the statue of *The Photographer*, another piece of public art. The statue is described on the photographers' plates.

Sesquicentenary pavement plaques continue down the Terrace, and the one for 1913 commemorates Winthrop Hackett, longtime editor of the *West Australian*, and major benefactor of the University of Western Australia (see Walk 13). On your left is the impressive **QV1 Building |7|**, with its angled sunshading tabs down the sides and its great curving glass canopy. Designed by Harry Seidler, QV1 won the Commercial category in the 1992 National Architecture Awards. The interior is column free and it's one of the most energy efficient buildings in Australia. Go in, and through the gigantic plain, angular foyer, through to a desert grove of palm trees with waterfall. You get an interesting perspective by looking up, past the palms to the top of the building. Continue across the courtyard to Hay Street. Directly opposite is the recently restored 'wedding cake' Melbourne Hotel (with toilets). The interior has understated Federation era elegance, with a timber staircase leading up to the accommodation and first floor balcony.

Go along Hay Street back towards the city centre. This next block has several groups of interesting and attractive two storey frontages on either side—some restored, others awaiting demolition or rescue. A new thirty-two level hotel has been approved for the right hand side, while retaining and restoring Dynon's China Hall and the Bank of NSW buildings.

Pass the entry to Shafto Lane on the left and enter the Cloisters Arcade on the right. Go through the arcade and down the escalator into the shade of a grand old Port Jackson Fig tree. Immediately on the right is a splendid little Tudor Gothic brick building, the **Cloisters |8|**, with a descriptive plaque at the front. This was originally Bishop Hale's Collegiate School and was designed by Richard Jewell again. It features some attractive decorative features, with Flemish Bond brickwork and diamond designs at the front, and an oriel window above the Bishop's coat of arms. Note that all three adjacent modern buildings have been constructed in brick to complement the Cloisters. Behind is Mt Newman House, the mining company that preserved and restored the Cloisters. To the left is London House, with another attractive foyer, and No. 190 St Georges Terrace, to the right, has a display of Perth Mint artefacts.

Go along the Terrace, passing the pavement plaque to Eileen Joyce the great international pianist, and then left up King Street to Hay Street.

You are now outside **His Majesty's Theatre** |9|, one of Perth's jewels, and recognised as the finest Edwardian theatre in Australia. The theatre and associated hotel were built where open air concerts and variety shows had previously been performed—on a grassy patch. The first performance was *The*

Forty Thieves by Pollard's Opera Company, on Christmas Eve 1904. Since then, most of WA's local and visiting artists have performed here. One of the Western Australia Government's most enlightened decisions was, in 1979, to rescue and restore what was then a badly fading gem. Go into the foyer where Friends of His Majesty's will provide information on the theatre and conduct ad hoc tours, excluding backstage. The official full scale tour (at a price) is on Thursdays. There are spacious public toilets, and on the ground floor is the Café Maj, where the original hotel was located. The theatre has a resident archivist, and a major collection of memorabilia associated with artists (such as Dame Nellie Melba and Pavlova) and productions that have visited the state over the years. There are frequent exhibitions of this material in the ground or first floor foyers.

Come out of His Majesty's and turn right to the nearby corner, where there's a photograph showing how the exterior originally looked. Cross to the corner diagonally opposite, and look back at His Majesty's to appreciate the opulent exterior. There is still a chance that the two tiers of balconies which extended around both sides of the theatre will eventually be restored. They, and many others in Perth, were removed because of public safety fears.

Continue along **King Street |10|**. This stretch of the street is one of Perth's finest and trendiest precincts. On both sides, elegant two and three-storey buildings have been refurbished and tizzied up to create cafés, boutiques, and galleries. The street and pavements have been modified to be more walker-friendly. Each building has its own little plaque, giving information on its style and previous uses.

Cross over Murray Street. In this section of King Street the buildings are larger and heavier, reflecting the fact that they were originally warehouses. Each building has an explanatory plaque, and some still have the protruding wooden beams that enabled goods to be hoisted to the upper floors.

The walk finishes at Wellington Street. The bus station is across the road, and the railway station is a block and a half away to the right.

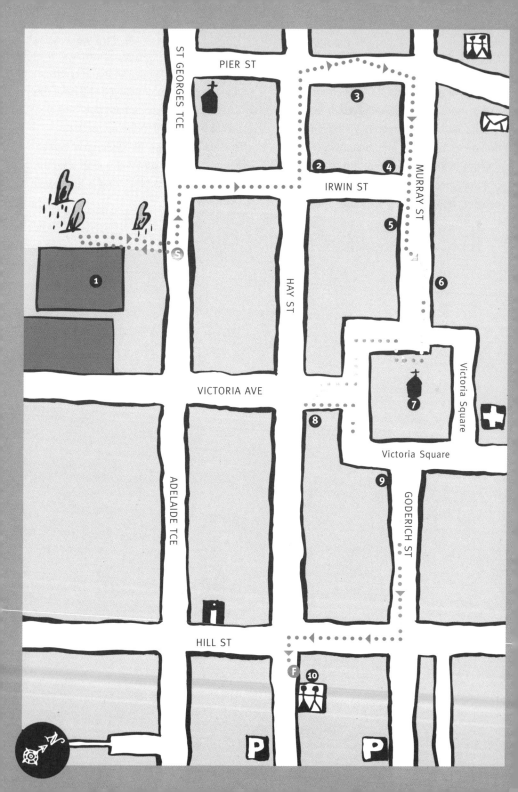

PIER ST

ST GEORGES TCE

3

2   4

IRWIN ST

MURRAY ST

5

S

6

1

HAY ST

Victoria Square

VICTORIA AVE

7

8

Victoria Square

9

ADELAIDE TCE

GODERICH ST

HILL ST

F

10

N

P   P

City East

Serving the people—churches, theatres, hospitals, fire stations and the Mint

Start

Entry to pedestrian underpass at No.16 St Georges Terrace. Walking distance from city centre, or any buses travelling east along St Georges Terrace, to the Victoria Avenue stop.

Finish

Corner Hay and Hill streets. Any buses travelling along Hay Street, and the Red CAT to the city centre.

Length/Time

2.3 km/about 2 hours

Wheelchairs

Generally good access. Go straight to Irwin Street from Ⓢ.

This can best be described as a service area, with some of the services going back to the earliest days of the colony.

The region around Victoria Square is especially important. This high point (everything is relative) along Perth's sandy spine is home to a remarkable series of Roman Catholic buildings, including one of the city's largest collections from the 19th century.

Across the square is Perth's oldest and largest teaching hospital. Other major service buildings include both the old and new fire stations, the Perth Concert Hall, sundry theatres and the Perth Mint.

Walk key

1. Perth Concert Hall | 2. St Georges Hall | 3. Salvation Army Headquarters | 4. Young Australia League | 5. Perth Fire Station | 6. Moreton Bay Fig | 7. St Marys Cathedral | 8. St John's Procathedral | 9. Convent of Mercy | 10. Perth Mint

Walk along the underpass which leads to the entrance of the **Perth Concert Hall** |1|, completed in 1973. It's a reinforced concrete structure which won an award of excellence from the Concrete Institute of Australia. It has some of the best acoustics in Australia, and can seat up to 2,300 people on three levels. Go through the doors directly in front. The box office is on the left, and an enquiry desk (and toilets). Ask about access into the auditorium. This is where the West Australian Symphony Orchestra performs most of its concerts throughout the year, and also the venue for many visiting singers and bands. The foyers and external corridors are sometimes used for exhibitions.

Leave through one of the doors either side of the circular staircase, and cross the terrace for an attractive view into Government House Gardens (see Walk 1). Walk back toward the underpass, but mount the staircase just before the entrance. This leads on to the northern forecourt, a bare expanse of brick paving. Cross this toward St Georges Terrace, and on reaching the pavement look back to get a good perspective of the Concert Hall.

A commemorative plaque is set into the pavement right by the Concert Hall sign. It was the first of a series of 150, laid to celebrate the first 150 years of Western Australia (1829–1979), and is dedicated to Captain James Stirling, who established the colony and became its first Governor.

Turn left, walk along the footpath to the next traffic lights, passing the plaque for 1830, marking the work of John Septimus Roe, who as Surveyor-General was responsible for the layout of the city as we now see it. Walk past the driveway into Government House grounds, to the pedestrian crossing, and cross St Georges Terrace to proceed up the right side of Irwin Street. On the left corner is Anzac House, home of the Returned Services League, and behind it the monolithic concrete structure of the Central Law Courts. This was the first, and temporary, site for the infant University of Western Australia. World War I intervened, so it was eighteen years later that it finally moved to its home in Crawley (see Walk 13). The original Irwin Street building has been reconstructed and now sits in the University grounds as home to the Cricket Club.

At the next traffic lights, cross the intersection, Hay Street. In front of you is another massive concrete structure, this time the modern Perth Central Fire Station. An interesting plaque outside its main entrance commemorates the burial of a 'Stone for Peace'. Turn left and cross Irwin Street to a rather sad Greek facade, the remnants of **St Georges Hall** |2|. Built in 1879 this was Perth's first purpose built theatre, and was transformed into a public open space in 1995. Both the sides of the portico and the statue/seat in the garden show replicas of old programmes. The rotunda just behind features the tragedy and comedy theatrical masks, and is part of the adjacent coffee house.

Continue along Hay Street, opposite the Kings Hotel and past the oriental frontage of one of Perth's oldest Chinese restaurants, the Canton. At the intersection with Pier Street, look left to the plain exterior of the 1950s style Playhouse Theatre, half way down the block. The Playhouse was supposed to have been demolished some twenty years ago but its long-promised replacement, a lyric arts theatre, has yet to appear. The interior has been revamped a few times, and it's now home to the Perth Theatre Company. Turn right into Pier Street, and cross over to the front of the Sebel Hotel. Look across the road to No. 50, a four storey red and white citadel built in heroic style and 'Erected to the Glory of God' when it was the **Salvation Army Headquarters |3|**. Walk up Pier Street to the next intersection passing the Miss Maud Swedish Hotel and Restaurant, one of Perth's best known eating houses. Diagonally opposite is the former Government Printer's Office, a beautifully proportioned Free Classical design, built in 1891–94.

Turn right, cross Pier Street and walk along Murray Street, across the road from the Printers, noting the iron crowns set on top of the tiny domes. Halfway along the block is No. 65, an unprepossessing structure, which houses another of Perth's theatres. It's currently the Yirra Yaakin Noongar (Aboriginal) Theatre. A little further on is No. 45, the **Young Australia League |4|** building, with a grand sandstone portico. As the YAL is no longer the power it once was (the foundation stone was laid by Australian Prime Minister Billy Hughes), it has had to sell its heritage listed building. It

Opening Times

Perth Concert Hall:
Mon–Sat 8.30am–5.30pm.
Old Perth Fire Station Museum:
Mon–Fri 10am–3pm.
Royal Perth Hospital Museum:
Wed and Thurs 9am–2pm.
St John's Procathedral Latin Mass:
Sun 11am.
Perth Mint: Open Mon–Fri 9am–4pm; other days 9am–1pm. Historical walks and gold pours hourly ($5 admission fee).

Refreshments

There are numerous cafés, restaurants and hotels on or near the route.

has been able to retain part of the ground floor though, which is being converted to a museum, containing such peculiar memorabilia as the presidential wreath from Teddy Roosevelt's inauguration as US President (he worked on the Western Australia goldfields before this), and stuffed moose and goat heads. If you're allowed, go through the great wooden inner doors, in their stone portals all set about with brass coats of arms of the states and Commonwealth. It may be possible to view the splendid old hall, with its timber floor and stained glass windows depicting heroes of the Empire. The YAL also owned a property in the hills, now converted to the Araluen Botanic Park (see Walk 25).

Outside again, continue east along Murray Street across Irwin Street, to the old **Perth Fire Station |5|,** This was built in 1899 to replace the undercroft of the Perth Town Hall (see Walk 1), which until then had been the base for the Perth Volunteer Fire Brigade. It was used until 1979 when the new station was opened right behind it. It's now a Museum and Fire Safety Education Centre. Entry is free and well worthwhile. Inside are some lovely, gleaming red Dennis fire engines and a Manual Fire Appliance that arrived in Fremantle in 1856. Up the splendid wooden stairs, there's an old spiral staircase, a fireman's pole, and public toilets. When you come out, cross the road for a full appreciation of this ornate, idiosyncratic building. You expect to see the old, concertina wooden doors, but not an ornate colonnade, nor

'The Strike' – *a statue celebrating the discovery of gold at Coolgardie.*

decorative plaster features such as fireman's helmets set among oak leaves.

The Royal Perth Hospital (RPH) complex starts here. Two of the early buildings are half hidden behind an enormous, heritage listed **Moreton Bay Fig |6|,** which spreads right across Murray Street. Kirkland House, with its double-storey wooden balcony, was built in 1909 as the Nurses' Home, while the second building was the original RPH Administration building dating from 1894. A driveway between these buildings leads to the RPH Museum, with an interesting collection of memorabilia and old photos, open only twice a week. The original 1850s Colonial Hospital still exists, but is hidden within a jumble of other, later buildings. The massive current hospital runs along the left side of Victoria Square just down the road.

This was originally designated Church Square and, being the high point of central Perth, was set aside for the establishment's Church of England. The early Anglicans did not, however, fancy the long, sandy trudge from the tiny town centre and decided to stay where their 'Rush' Church had been built. The Roman Catholics then said 'thank you very much'. Occupying the centre of the square is **St Mary's Cathedral |7|**.

If you stand on the pavement at the entrance to the square you can see that the cathedral is actually made up of two buildings. The nearer, smaller portion, built between 1863 and 1865, has a small steeple with gargoyles at the corners. The newer portion dates from 1925–26, and starts partway along, protruding on both sides, especially the right, showing bare concrete and reinforcing rods. The intention was obviously to continue this newer church to replace the old one, but funds were not available. Plans have recently been announced to begin completion in 2001. There's considerable deterioration in the old part, but there will be attempts to retain some of it.

Cross over the road towards the cathedral, noting that the traffic flow in the Square is one way, anti-clockwise. Go to the right-hand side, to an entrance into the older west end. Inside the cathedral proper note the low moulded ceilings, due to the

existence of a gallery. Just on the left is a bell, made in 1676 in Compostella in Spain, and brought here by Dom Salvado, the founder of New Norcia. Move further down the nave, and the splendour of the new building is apparent, with glorious, soaring vaulted arches and superb stained glass windows. Come out of the cathedral and back across the road to a very rare series of four identical old brick and iron cottages, now occupied by various Catholic agencies. Follow the footpath around to the left and behind a hedge is the large white Catholic Presbytery, originally the Bishop's Palace. The building was started in the 1850s, with the colonnading added in the 1920s. All the ground floor windows have attractive stained glass designs.

Cross over the street coming up from the right, Victoria Avenue, and turn down it for a few metres to the small, simple, white plastered **St John's Procathedral |8|**. A window in the door allows you to look inside this, the oldest of all the Catholic buildings here (dating from 1844), to see its wooden floors and ceiling. A Latin Mass is said here every Sunday. Immediately behind the tiny procathedral and running at right angles to it is the original Convent of Mercy built in 1848. It is a plain (there was no money for frills in those days), double-storey, iron-roofed cream building.

Go back up the hill, and on the corner of the Square there's a much grander two-storey limestone building with a plaque from 1895. It's now a part of Mercedes College, a Catholic girls' school.

Proceeding round the Square to the right, you pass an open grassed area before turning left past the Church of the Immaculate Conception, a comparative newcomer from 1924. At the next intersection, with Goderich Street, is the **Convent of Mercy |9|**. The brass plaque reads 'Sisters of Mercy 1846' but is misleading. The building was constructed in 1871 to the style of a traditional Irish convent, and the balcony added in the 1880s. Stand back to admire some of the features—tuck pointed red brickwork, the wooden balcony with ironwork balustrade supported on turned wooden posts, unusual brick designs in the gable, and the triple chimneys.

Follow the Convent round the corner into Goderich Street, to the first double gates. Behind the carport is an interesting wing, made of glowing multicoloured bricks that came out of the Queen's Garden brickworks in the late 19th century. A series of other brick buildings, all part of either the Sisters of Mercy Convent or Mercedes College, stretch the rest of the block to Hill Street, while on the opposite side of the road is the Perth Dental Hospital, followed by the tall, ugly Jewell House, a YMCA hotel/hostel.

Turn right into Hill Street. Across the road is a spiked steel fence and behind it a stained limestone building with two tall brick chimneys. This is part of the **Perth Mint |10|**, and the chimneys are from the days when gold was regularly smelted here.

The next intersection is Hay Street again, and opposite is the Grosvenor, a traditional Federation style balconied hotel. Meals,

drinks and toilets are available here. Cross to the left over Hill Street and straight along to the entrance of the Mint.

Set well back from Hay Street, it stands foursquare, solid and dependable, as though to emphasise its financial importance and integrity. It was built of Rottnest Island limestone to a design by the great colonial architect, George Temple Poole. The stone walls gleam beyond flowering shrubs and green lawns. The high iron fence merely provides a picture frame for a Grand Old Lady.

Perth Mint opened in 1899 as a branch of the Royal Mint, to refine the vast amount of gold pouring out of Western Australia's goldfields. It's now one of the world's top producers of precious metal coinage, for Australia and other countries, and is thought to be the world's oldest mint operating from its original premises.

Pass through the guardhouse (public toilets are on the left hand side), and straight ahead is *'The Strike'*, a statue commemorating the first discovery of gold at Coolgardie. Inside the mint is a shop where bullion and precious metal items can be viewed or purchased, and current bullion prices are displayed. There's also a museum area at the back, with access down the passage past the reception desk. There's a fee to enter, which includes the guided historic walk and gold pouring demonstration.

The best option is probably to take the hourly historic walk. This gives interesting information on WA's gold mining industry as well as the Mint, and it is timed to coincide with the gold pour. The same batch of gold has been melted and poured, 36 times a week, ever since 1990. As an indication of the quality controls of the process, the gold bar still weighs 200 ounces (worth about $100,000), and still has a purity of over 99.95%.

After the gold pour, visitors have the chance to watch the real activities of the Mint. While the actual production areas are kept under tight security, large armoured glass windows allow visitors to watch what's happening. There's a wide range of nuggets and coins on display, and these are the real thing, with an estimated value of $2,500,000. Surprisingly there are no give away samples. This is the end of the walk. The CAT bus stop is in Hay Street on the other side of Hill Street.

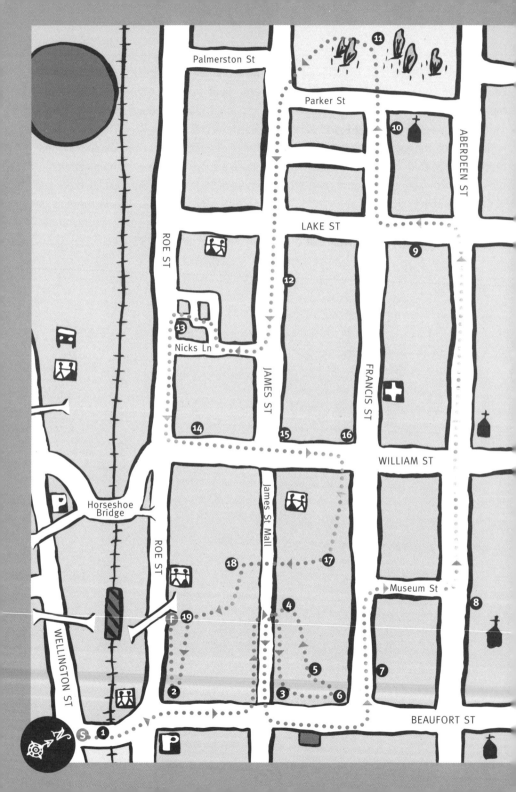

Northbridge
The other side of the tracks

Start
Barrack Street Bridge,
corner of Wellington Street.

Finish
Art Gallery of Western Australia.

Length/Time
4 km/3.5–4.5 hours

Wheelchairs
Wheelchair users will need
to make a short detour
to reach the PICA.

Walk key

1. Barrack Street Bridge | 2. Police
Courts | 3. Jubilee Building | 4. Hackett
Hall | 5. Old Gaol | 6. Museum and
Gallery of Arts | 7. Swan Barracks |
8. St Johns Lutheran Church |
9. Re Store | 10. Greek Orthodox
Cathedral of Saints Constantine and
Helene | 11. Russell Square | 12. Chung
Wah Association Building | 13. Chinatown |
14. Kakulas Brothers | 15. Brass
Monkey | 16. Loreto Bell Tower |
17. Alexander Library | 18. Perth Institute
of Contemporary Arts (PICA) |
19. Art Gallery of Western Australia

Separated from the city by the railway line, Northbridge has also been the other side of the law. For years this was the centre for brothels, SP bookmakers and illegal gambling dens.

Even today, when it's become respectable as Perth's major restaurant and night club district, there's still the occasional feel of lawlessness.

Northbridge has major cultural and multicultural links. Sometimes known as the Cultural Precinct, it houses the Art Gallery, Museum, and State Library—in a range of historic and modern buildings.

Partly because of its separation from Perth, Northbridge has been the focus for various migrant waves. First the Chinese, then Greeks and Italians, and more recently the Vietnamese —and they've all left their mark.

The first thing to separate North Perth, as it was known originally, from Perth City, was a series of lakes and wetlands which covered much of the land north of the city. When these were drained the reclaimed land provided an easy location for the railway.

The **Barrack Street Bridge |1|** was built in 1894, replacing an earlier wooden version, and runs at an angle to connect with Beaufort Street. The bridge has some intriguing street lamps with black swan insignia. It once sheltered Australian author Henry Lawson who came to Perth with his bride during the Gold Rush, and unable to find any accommodation, camped under the bridge. Cross over the bridge, and then over Roe Street to the old **Police Courts |2|**. This, like many other buildings in the Cultural Precinct, was designed in 1905 by Western Australia's Principal Architect, Hillson Beasley. It housed various courts and offices until 1982, when it became part of the art gallery. The interior is explored at a later point in this walk.

Continue along the Beaufort Street frontage of the courts, as far as the James Street Mall on the left, opposite the Court Hotel. Facing you in the mall is the curved **Jubilee Building (3)**, which, in 1897, commemorated Queen Victoria's sixty years on the throne.

The arches and supporting columns are unusual, being of Rottnest limestone, and were originally open, but the effect was lost when they were enclosed. This building was designed by colonial architect George Temple Poole as the first stage of a planned cultural centre.

Go along the mall and past the Jubilee main entrance, which has also been bricked off. Entry to the entire museum complex is now through the tall glass structure that links the Jubilee Building with the stone and brick building beyond, **Hackett Hall |4|**. The hall was a Beasley design and, while it shows similarities to Poole's work with its arches and cupolas, has deliberate variations. The floor levels are different and Hackett Hall protrudes 30 feet further. Apparently Beasley planned a new frontage which would have totally hidden Poole's work. Poole was not impressed. The new glass foyer solves the problem. Being glass it does not impinge visually on its neighbours, and allows the **Old Gaol |5|** behind it to be seen.

Immediately behind you, on the other side of the mall, is the Arts Gallery Administration Building, built in 1905 as the Police Barracks before becoming the Central Police Station. Unfortunately, it's not open to the public.

Go into the museum through the glass foyer; entry is free. There are several sections of special interest. Turn left into Hackett Hall, named after Sir John Winthrop Hackett, the principal benefactor of the University of Western Australia (see Walk 13). The ground floor houses the Discovery Centre while the upper levels have a display featuring Western Australia's land and people. The building was originally part of the public library, and has recently been refurbished, uncovering the galleries and magnificent ceiling, which can now be clearly seen and admired.

Return through the glass foyer and into the Jubilee Building, with its three levels housing: dinosaurs, the mammals gallery, and a splendid butterfly collection on the ground floor just behind the enclosed arches. These areas lead off into the foyer which is dominated by a double staircase and an enormous, incongruous stuffed bison. The foyer, and the display spaces beyond, are part of the Museum and Gallery of Arts building from 1907, another Beasley design. The lower gallery is used to display travelling exhibitions, while the vaulted Hellenic Gallery is on the first floor.

Next to the foyer stairs is a door which leads into a small open courtyard, and directly opposite is the oldest (and best concealed) building of the complex, the Old Gaol. Note the high Georgian entrance, which probably came from a Royal Engineers pattern book.

The gaol was convict built in 1856, well away from the settlers in their own little world along St Georges Terrace. It was built on relatively high ground clear of the nearby low lying swampy areas, but this meant it was visible from Perth, which caused later complaints. In 1891 the gaol was converted to a Geological Museum, and in the 1970s totally renovated.

The interior has displays from early Western Australian history, including a series of views from Mt Eliza (see Walk 7), and information on John Forrest who had a

Opening Times

Art Gallery of Western Australia: daily 10am–5pm.
WA Museum: Mon–Fri 10.30am–5pm (including public holidays); Sat 1pm–5pm.
Alexander Library: Mon–Thurs 9am–9.45pm; Fri 9am–5.30pm; Sat and Sun 10am–5.30pm.
Perth Institute of Contemporary Arts: Tues–Sun 11am–8pm.

Refreshments

The art gallery, museum and library all have cafés. Otherwise there are hundreds of restaurants and cafés, of every type imaginable, throughout the area.

great influence on Western Australia's development. Its wooden floors, ceiling and catwalks are noteworthy.

Exit the gaol, go around the courtyard with its series of rock exhibits to the two other buildings in the complex. The multi-storey modern structure dates from 1970–71 and houses the Aboriginal and Marine galleries. At the end of the courtyard is the Roe Street Cottage, a partial reconstruction using much of the original material of an 1863 building. There's even a garden behind the cottage. The way out is back through the glass foyer.

Turn left, back past the Jubilee Building, and cross over Beaufort Street (one-way traffic) to the City Police Station, which is housed in Curtin House, named after the wartime Prime Minister. Look back across the road at the Jubilee Building and the adjoining **Museum and Gallery of Arts |6|**. Once again, Beasley's design is very attractive but doesn't really complement the first house on the block, the Jubilee Building.

Continue past Delaney Gallery and the Labor Centre (Head Office of the Australian Labor Party in Western Australia) and then turn left into Francis Street. On the left is the modern museum building, and opposite is the **Swan Barracks |7|** (now Swan College) not quite dominated by its later brick surrounds. This impressive limestone pile, with its British coat of arms, was another Beasley creation, though the third floor is a later addition. Walk to Museum Street and turn right. The double storey building with iron lace balconies on the left

'The Caller' *outside the Art Gallery.*

was originally No. 27, now renumbered as No. 1, since the rest of the street behind you was swallowed up by the Cultural Precinct.

At the top of the road is the lovely little **St Johns Lutheran Church |8|**, built in 1936 using lateritic rock from the Darling Range. Go left here into Aberdeen Street, past one of the buildings of the Central Metropolitan College of TAFE (Technical and Further Education). Much of the area to the right has been cleared or otherwise affected by the construction of a cross city traffic tunnel, due for completion in 2000.

Continue along Aberdeen Street, over the major one way William Street, and into the start of the restaurant belt. On the right are three old brick and iron houses, with 1860 rears and 1890 frontages. These are to be restored as part of the tunnel urban renewal process. The Aberdeen Hotel further on is one of several hotels in the area, while the large European Foods Centre reflects the ethnic influences here.

Turn left into Lake Street, and just round the corner is the **Re Store |9|**. The Re family were among the very early Italian migrants to Western Australia and first opened a store in Fremantle, before shifting to North Perth. It's still very much a family enterprise, with the fourth generation now in control. The flow of Italians into this area was such that it was known for a time as 'Little Italy'. The influence can still be seen, not only in the Re Store but also in the names of other shops and restaurants.

Turn right at the next intersection into Francis Street, round the modern mock Tudor British pub. At the end of the block is the red brick **Greek Orthodox Cathedral of Saints Constantine and Helene |10|**, built in traditional Byzantine style. If the church is open, the murals, icons and altar screen are worth seeing.

Across the road is an unusual house. It was probably built in the 1890s, using the pastel coloured bricks that were typical of the era. It was for some years the residence of the Greek priest, but is now used to train hospitality students. The park opposite is **Russell Square |11|**, which has recently been upgraded. It was known for a time as 'Parco de Sospiri' (Park of Sighs), because the Italian migrants used to meet here to dream of home and family. Cross over to the edge of the square, and look back at the cathedral, and the Hellenic Community Centre next door. Greeks were another group who established their base in North Perth, and it is interesting to note that both they and the Italians used to meet here. Go to the copper roofed rotunda in the middle of the park, a pleasant spot for a brief rest, being cool and breezy with four highly individual fountains around it. The four designs portray the influences of Europe, Asia, the environment and leisure upon today's Northbridge.

Walk left through the park to James Street. The area around Russell Square, like the park, was once rather seedy, but has been revitalised with the development of several attractive apartment blocks. Off to the right is the rear of the Metropole Nightclub, with its three jet engine style exhausts. Go left along James Street, over two small roads and Lake Street.

Part way along the next block, at No. 128, is the colourful **Chung Wah Association Building |12|**. This was the first ethnic clubhouse in Perth, and catered for its members' social and educational needs. The first Chinese arrived as indentured 'coolie' labour, and some restricted immigration was allowed in the late 19th century. North Perth was where they congregated, some working market gardens in the vicinity (around the old lake beds).

A little further on is Nick's Lane, leading off to the right. Go halfway down and then right into a small lane/car park. Turn left into Chung Wah Lane, which leads into the **Chinatown |13|** development. This has several Chinese restaurants and an impressive pagoda type gateway that opens on to Roe Street, with the railway just beyond. Roe Street was infamous for its brothels and known as the 'Street of Shame'. It was close to the city, on the wrong side of the tracks, and there were lots of single male migrants. Apparently the queues stretched down the road on paydays. Go left, past yet more restaurants, and a tinware manufacturer (Nos. 30–36) in an old workshop.

The next intersection is William Street, and provides an excellent view of the great loop of the Horseshoe Bridge with Perth Railway Station behind it. The railway had been built when another north–south road link was needed. The only way to provide a bridge without massive embankments either side was to curve the road up and over in a horseshoe shape.

Turn left into William Street. Nos. 183–187 house the **Kakulas Brothers |14|** store, one of the oldest Greek shops in the city and one which has barely changed over the years. Wooden floors, shelves, counters and boxes hold an intriguing variety of nuts, cereals, seeds, coffees, pasta, dried fruit, sweets and spices. The atmosphere and the smells are amazing.

Carry on up William Street to the next intersection, with James Street. Opposite is the **Brass Monkey |15|**, originally the Great Western Hotel, built in 1897. This hotel is remarkable for having kept its domed tower and iron lace balconies. It was recently renovated. Inside there are original floors and ceilings, and the first floor balcony is a great spot for a rest, a view, and a drink. When you can drag yourself away from here, continue along William Street. The Rechabite Hall, across the road at No. 224, is another reminder of a different era, when friendly societies provided educational and other support services. The Rechabites were also a temperance society—there was probably a need here but perhaps not many takers.

The near corner of Francis Street has the **Loreto Bell Tower |16|**. This remnant of Loreto Convent was moved to this spot from Claremont in 1991, and provides a welcome distraction from the bulk of the Australian Tax Office just behind. On the opposite corner is the Britannia Youth Hostel, once a hotel, with an attractive octagonal witch's hat tower and broad band of coloured tiles. To appreciate the line and scale of the Britannia, cross over William Street (one way traffic), then walk along Francis Street.

The building on the left is part of Perth TAFE (seen earlier in the walk), with the **Alexander** (or State) **Library |17|** opposite it. Take the steps or ramp down and go inside. The ground floor has a large range of international newspapers, and there's often an exhibition opposite the café. The third floor has the Battye Library, which houses much of the state's archival material. Go through the foyer to the opposite door, and then half right past the abstract black and white sculpture (meaningfully called *Gate 2: Coalesce*), and down the steps to the square towered building. This 'Government School' was the Perth Boys' School, built in 1896 by Poole, and is now the **Perth Institute of Contemporary Arts (PICA) |18|**, which houses exhibitions and occasional performances.

Please note that the courtyard areas of the Cultural Centre, either side of PICA and across to the Art Gallery are being revamped during 1999–2000. New levels and malls are being created, so some of the descriptions here may be inaccurate.

With your back to PICA, turn right and go up the nearby steps. There's a good view of Hackett Hall to the left. Turn right towards the **Art Gallery of Western Australia |19|**. Part way along is another outdoor sculpture, the tall bronze *The Caller*, dedicated to victims of torture. The Art Gallery building was opened in 1979, and awarded the RAIA Bronze Medal in 1983. The design was based on a hexagon, to avoid 90 degree corners. A linkway runs through to the

Centenary Galleries, housed in the old Police Courts, whose exterior was seen at the beginning of the walk.

Entry to the gallery is free, except for special exhibitions. The usual highlights include Western Australian and other Historical Art (both based in the Centenary Galleries), Aboriginal and Contemporary Art, and Craft and Design. The Aboriginal collection has a wide range of artists, styles and materials and includes both totems and paintings.

The linkway to the Centenary Galleries is on the ground floor. The old court rooms have fans idly circling beneath superb pressed tin ceilings. Court No. 1 has the strange touch of various art works set among the original dark, heavy jarrah court furniture. The old main entrance, which opened out on to Beaufort Street, has some excellent leadlights, including a stained glass coat of arms. Halfway up the jarrah staircase is one of Western Australia's best known paintings: *The Foundation of Perth*, showing Mrs Dance about to cut down a jarrah tree to mark the town's establishment. The walk finishes at the art gallery exit.

Walk key

1. Parliament House |
2. Constitutional Centre |
3. Old Observatory |
4. Meerilinga | 5. St Mary's Anglican Church |
6. Kingsway Gardens |
7. Edith Cowan Memorial |
8. Jacob's Ladder |
9. Mount Street

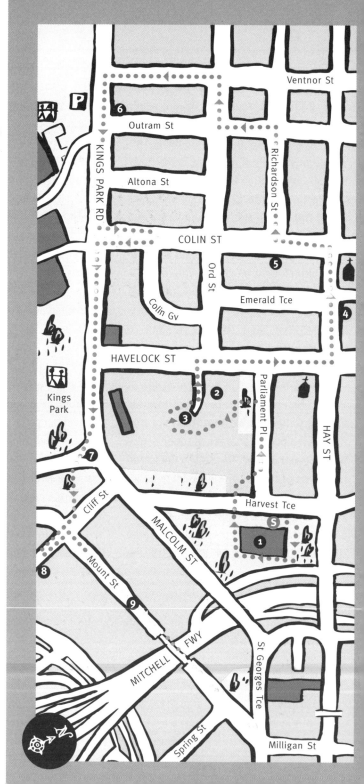

West Perth

Life on the edge (of town)

Start

Outside Parliament House,
opposite the intersection
of Harvest Terrace and
Parliament Place.
Take the Red CAT to the
Parliament stop, or any bus
travelling west from St Georges
Terrace or Hay Street
(ask for Parliament House).

Finish

Mount Street/St George
Terrace intersection.
Any bus going east along
St Georges Terrace will bring
you back to the city centre.

Length/Time

4 km/2.5 hours

Wheelchairs

Steps at Parliament House and
the Constitutional Centre can
be bypassed with short
diversions. Mount Street
is very steep.

West Perth is the seat of government, and probably the professional centre of Perth. Doctors, lawyers, dentists, consultants, and restaurateurs have all hung their shingles here.

After Western Australia achieved self-government in 1890 there was a need for a proper Parliament House. It was built here, overlooking the city. About the same time West Perth became a desirable residential area, and the wealthy built large mansions adjacent to Kings Park. As times changed, the mansion grounds were subdivided, and then converted to surgeries, other professional offices, or restaurants. There are a few gems left, although many have been replaced by mostly low rise office or apartment blocks.

Western Australia's **Parliament House** |1| is a badly flawed compromise between design, function and budget. A design competition was held in 1900, but none of the entries came within the limited budget. Accordingly the Public Works department, under Government Architect John Grainger, produced a simpler, cheaper version. Even then, only a small part of that design, excluding the wings and central dome, could be afforded. This resulted in the Donnybrook sandstone frontage facing Harvest Terrace, rather than down St Georges Terrace. Nothing further happened until 1958, when a reworking of the original design produced the facade now seen from the city. The interior has remained cramped and badly ventilated.

Face Parliament House, turn left down Harvest Terrace, and right into the driveway signed 'Parliament House Main Entrance'. Pass through a leafy grove into a broad open courtyard dominated by a single magnificent towering lemon-scented gum. The terrace provides a view over ponds and fountains, the cavernous freeway, and the full length of St Georges Terrace – past the relic of the Barracks Arch – and right to Perth Water. (Toilets are on the next level down.) Turn to look at Parliament House. The squared-off facade of 1964 is topped by the Western Australia coat of arms and three flagpoles. If three flags are flying Parliament is in session that day, and the public galleries open. Both chambers, the Legislative Assembly and Legislative Council, are well-proportioned,

attractive spaces with wood panelling (from NSW!) and ornate ceilings. Phone (9222 7222) beforehand to check the public gallery opening times.

Continue around the House and up the steps at the side back to Harvest Terrace. Take the pedestrian crossing to Solidarity Park, built (illegally) by Trade Union members during the 1997 'Workers Embassy' protest against Western Australian industrial legislation. Continue diagonally across the car park to the street misleadingly called Parliament Place.

About 150 metres along Parliament Place, take the pathway on the left, up to the attractive long, low limestone and brick building. This is now the **Constitutional Centre** |2| but was originally the Perth High School when opened in 1914. This was the successor to Bishop Hale's Collegiate School (see Walk 3), which, renamed Hale School, moved out to the suburban spaces of Wembley Downs in 1961. The building was renovated in 1997 (receiving a Western Australia award) and is now home to both the Constitutional Centre of Western Australia and the Electoral Education Centre. Entry is free. A superb movie style hologram gives an entertaining overview of WA's constitutional history, and you can hear the maiden speech of Edith Cowan, Australia's first woman parliamentarian, elected for West Perth in 1921.

Go out the front door, turn right, go around the building, up the paved path and through the gates to the National Trust Headquarters, which are in the **Old Obser-**

vatory |3|. The colonial architect, George Temple Poole, designed this purpose-built Astronomer's Residence in 1896. A separate domed building, which housed the telescope and actually was the observatory, was demolished in 1963, when the observatory moved to Bickley, to avoid the increasing impact of the city lights.

The elevated position here was chosen to give clear views of the river and the Darling Range, as well as the stars, thus the circular verandahs. The square tower has its corners aligned with the cardinal points of the compass to help identify cloud and wind direction. The National Trust (Western Australia) will provide brief tours of the interior by appointment.

Walk around outside the building, and note the pleasing effect of the circles, triangles and squares incorporated into the design. Go down the drive, through the gates and left to Havelock Street. Turn right along the far side of the street. Nos. 29, 33 and 45 are examples of old houses converted to modern commercial uses, with varying levels of renovation and redevelopment. Across the road from No. 45 is the rather plain Seventh Day Adventist Church.

Continue to Hay Street where you can see, a little way down to the right, the unusual and neglected Entertainment House, its third floor being almost entirely corrugated iron. Turn left up Hay Street, West Perth's main thoroughfare. **Meerilinga** |4| is further along on the right side of the road, half hidden behind trees. This was one of Perth's finest houses, with a

Opening Times

Parliament House galleries: open sitting days only. Phone: (08) 9222 7222. **Constitutional Centre:** Tues–Sat 9.30am–4.30pm; Sun and Mon 12.30pm–4.30pm. **Old Observatory:** Mon–Fri 9am–4.30pm. For tours, phone National Trust: (08) 9321 6088. **Ross Memorial (Uniting) Church:** every second Thurs 12 noon–2pm; and Sun mornings. **St Mary's Anglican Church:** daily 9am–2pm.

Refreshments

Numerous restaurants and sandwich shops in Hay Street and throughout West Perth, excluding Kings Park Road.

three storey tower, timber balconies, oriel window and alternating red and cream decorative effects. This is home to the Meerilinga Young Children's Association.

The next intersection, with Colin Street, features the Ross Memorial (Uniting) Church. Built between 1916 and 1918, it replaced a nearby Presbyterian Church which was no longer big enough. Turn left into Colin Street, and walk to **St Mary's Anglican Church** |5|. The modern interior is cool and soothing, and there is a satisfying blend of traditional and contemporary stained glass windows.

Go into Richardson Street, directly opposite the church. Numerous old houses still exist here, showing a variety of styles and materials. No. 9 on the left is an excellent refurbishment while Nos. 17, 19, 22 and 24 are interesting and different types of duplex buildings.

At the next intersection, Outram Street, note the semi-detached town houses just to the right. Go left along Outram Street, passing the heavy mock-Tudor house at No. 34, to the intersection with Ord Street. Cross diagonally to the bungalow, with bullnose verandah and decorative plaster alcoves, half hidden behind its palm trees. Continue along Ord Street, to the corner of Ventnor Street where another verandahed house still shows style and repose. The tennis court (round the corner) is now a part-time car park!

Turn left into Ventnor Street, where No. 5 is one of the most elegant remaining mansions (though now an office). The tuck point brickwork, first floor balcony and turned posts have all been superbly refurbished, but where you might expect to find a grand internal staircase winding up to the first floor, none exists. Strangely, access is by the external stairs on the right.

Continue along Ventnor Street and left into Kings Park Road, an attractive boulevard with rosebushes in the central reservation, and the park itself on the other side. **Kingsway Gardens |6|**, at the Outram

The Old Observatory, now home to the National Trust.

Street intersection, is an older style apartment block with a distinctive green 'cap' — its water tank. The building is higher than the nearby Kings Park reservoir, so cannot rely on gravity feed. The gates opposite lead to the Tennis Club and the Lotteries Family Area (with café and toilets). Most of the Kings Park Road houses have been replaced by office blocks. Two exceptions are No. 34, which looks as though the owner is waiting for a developer, and No. 24 which has been well maintained.

Turn left into Colin Street, where the corner property has a nine storey apartment block under development. At the next intersection, No. 18 is one of West

Perth's grandest mansions, built in 1911. The original owner, Robert Law, was the builder of the Perth Mint and most of the jetties on the Western Australia coast, and the size and style of the house reflected his position and wealth. Return to Kings Park Road, turning left towards Havelock Street, and the offices of Argyle Diamonds, one of the world's major producers of diamonds. This is perhaps the most security-minded building in Perth.

Cross Havelock Street towards the pedestrian crossing. The large building on your left is Dumas House, a government office block. The design was selected by public competition in 1963, and was meant to be one of several such slab blocks in the area. No more were built, and this remains as an unfortunate anomaly. Also sad is the closure (for safety reasons) of the lookout which was on the top floor. Cross Kings Park Road and turn left towards the park entry. The clock tower in the middle of the road is the **Edith Cowan Memorial |7|**, built in 1934 to commemorate her work for the welfare of women, mothers and children.

Cross Fraser Avenue (the entry to Kings Park) and turn half right across the lawn toward the two tall apartment blocks. The circular one, known as the 'Thermos Flask', has been a landmark since the 1950s. Bellevue Terrace, off to the right, has superb views of Perth Water and the city (see Walk 7). Cross Bellevue Street and go down the short extension of Cliff Street. The lookout has views of the Narrows interchange, the river and South Perth.

Immediately below is **Jacob's Ladder |8|**, a thigh-challenging set of steps down to Mounts Bay Road.

Return to the Cliff Street roundabout and go down the right side of **Mount Street |9|**, a quiet, tree-lined residential avenue which has lost many of its original houses to apartment blocks. The first block on the right ('Wittenoom', No. 65) with its art deco effects, was a Marshall Clifton design from 1935, and you can see where two floors were added in 1984. This caused the building to sink some 300 centimetres and necessitated two steps down by the entrance.

Across the road are two striking Victorian town houses, with splendid iron lace balconies, though they've lost some of their views. Just below them is the interesting modern development of a highrise block which retained, and refurbished, the two old houses fronting Mount Street. The next house is a grand Victorian structure with tower and balcony, but it is now well concealed from the road. The lower section of Mount Street is less appealing, with most of the left hand side converted to flats and apartments, and much of the other side (with most of its views lost) going the same way.

At the bottom is a footbridge leading across the Mitchell Freeway. This offers a good close-up view of the constant traffic. Mount Street continues on the other side of the bridge, and soon leads to St Georges Terrace—with the city centre a short distance to the right. This is the end of the walk.

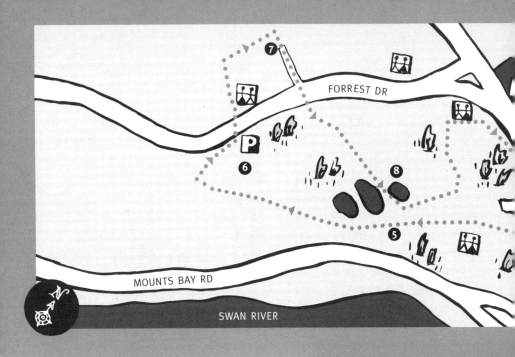

FORREST DR

MOUNTS BAY RD

SWAN RIVER

Walk key

1. South African War Memorial |
2. Covered Lookout | 3. Court of
Contemplation | 4. Anzac Bluff |
5. Rotunda | 6. Roe Memorial |
7. DNA Observation Tower |
8. Pioneer Women's Memorial
Fountain | 9. Statue of Lord John
Forrest | 10. Karri Log | 11. Queen
Victoria's Statue | 12. Display
Glasshouses

Start/Finish

Left side of the
main entrance to Kings Park,
at Fraser Avenue
(off Kings Park Road).
Buses leave the city westward
along St Georges Terrace–
Nos. 33, 102, 103, 104, 200,
202, 207, 208, 209. Catch
any of the same buses
back into town.

Length/Time

5 km/3–4 hours.

Wheelchairs

Several rough sections and
steps make this walk
unsuitable for wheelchair user

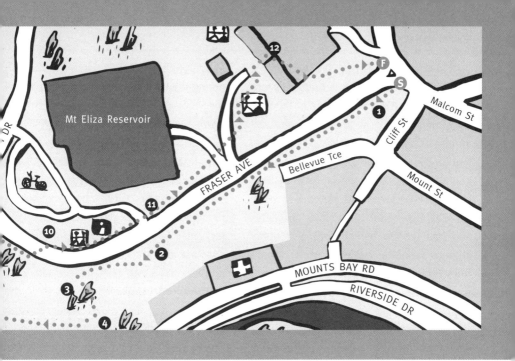

Walk No. 7

Kings Park
Perth's jewel

Kings Park occupies over 400 hectares of prime inner-city land, with the finest natural vantage point in the metropolitan area. A tall limestone scarp, Mt Eliza, juts out over the Swan River, giving superb, uninterrupted views of the city right across to the Darling Range.

It's not just the view. The bulk of the park is natural bush, with a major Botanic Garden which features much of Western Australia's rich plant heritage. Kings Park is where the wars of the 20th century, and the people who fought and died in them, are commemorated. The area also had great significance to the local Aboriginal people—and still has.

Look down Fraser Avenue. This is the tree lined avenue that leads into the park and it's a supurb vista. Immediately on the left is a small rotunda, built around a tree, which displays general information about the park, including details on guided walks and special events. Just behind it is an enormous, buttressed Moreton Bay Fig (haunt of rainbow lorikeets), and half hidden behind that is a rather strange memorial made of artillery shells from HMS *Queen Elizabeth*, a World War I warship. Next is the **South African War Memorial |1|**, with excellent bronzes portraying scenes from that conflict, the first war in which West Australians participated. The small surrounding garden contains plants native to South Africa, though many are now common here.

Return to Fraser Avenue, and note the plaques by each tree, commemorating the state's Centenary Committee of 1929 even though those worthy folk did not plant these trees. In 1898, lines of red flowering gums were planted here, and another set planted in 1929. The whole lot became diseased and were dug up in 1938, and the existing lemon-scented gums put in. On still evenings the scent is unmistakable.

Just to the left is a line of apartments and large houses. This is Bellevue Terrace, one of Perth's most exclusive and expensive addresses, with great views over the river and city. Many argue that this land should have been part of the park.

Continue along to the **covered lookout |2|**, an Education Centre, performance area and Aboriginal gallery. Go into the lookout, noting the US Navy 'thank you' plaque, and the Aboriginal motifs. The view straight down the escarpment overlooks the hospital and apartment blocks along Mounts Bay Road (the original waterline), and the Narrows Interchange. This convoluted swirl of roads, with interwoven areas of parkland, was constructed on land reclaimed from the bay, to link the city with Kwinana and Mitchell freeways. The fountains in the small lake on the left were designed to represent the stars of the Australian flag. The broad sweep of Perth Water is directly ahead (with the 'bump' of the Barrack Street Jetty on the left) separated from the city skyscrapers by another stretch of reclaimed land. South Perth is to the right, and the Darling Range on the horizon. Take the steps down to the gallery, which usually has an Artist in Residence. Aboriginal artefacts as well as pictures are on sale. The local Aboriginal people have several names for what we now call Kings Park including *Mooro Katta* (hill of significance) or *Ginunjkura* (looking a long way).

Walk up the sloping path opposite the gallery entrance to the Wishing Well, and on to the small, domed marble memorial, the George Leake Fountain. For much of the 19th century this level area was the site of a rifle range used by the Defence Volunteers. Turn right back towards Fraser Avenue, passing the mottled gum which is the 'Duke's Tree'.

Go past the main memorial entrance to the obelisk with a ball on top, the Jewish War

Memorial. A small service is held here every Anzac Day, after the main ceremony, and it is quite beautiful with the cantor singing.

Retrace your steps, noting the large 'Queen's Tree' (a river gum) on the right, and enter the **Court of Contemplation** |3|. The curving granite amphitheatre is a 'whispering wall' commemorating the major campaigns or battles in which West Australians were involved. Those of World War I are on the right, and of WWII on the left. There is a separate plaque on the left for the subsequent campaigns in Korea, Malaya, Borneo and Vietnam. Placed around the nearer flowerbeds are bronze tablets for the West Australians who between them won fifteen Victoria Crosses and two George Crosses in these conflicts.

Stand at the entrance to the amphitheatre to appreciate the site and layout. Go towards the Cenotaph, past the Flame of Remembrance and through the open grassed area, which is packed with people every year for the Dawn Service on Anzac Day (25 April). It's an eerie, yet stirring feeling to arrive in the dark and gradually realise that you're in the midst of a vast, silent crowd. Then the sun rises behind the Cenotaph, wreaths are laid and the 'Last Post' sounded. The butts of the rifle range had been here, and were only demolished in 1932, after the Cenotaph was completed. Go around to the back of the monument, where the names of the fallen are engraved, in the undercroft for WWI and outside for WWII. On the railing overlooking the river a plaque explains the name of **Anzac Bluff** |4|.

Opening Times

The park is never closed.

Guided walks: the Kings Park Volunteers run free daily walks (at 10am) through the Botanic Garden, or along the Heritage Walk, and in winter there are also Bush Walks or walks along the Wildflower Trail. For full details, phone: 9480 3600.

Display glasshouses: daily (except Tues) 10am–4pm.

Refreshments

Restaurant and kiosk within the park, and numerous water fountains.

Route Notes

Spring (August to October) is wildflower time, and there is a Wildflower Show for 10 days every September.

The commonly used name for this headland and the surrounding high land is Mt Eliza. Captain James Stirling, who founded the state of Western Australia, first sailed up the Swan River in 1827, and named this prominence after the wife of the Governor of New South Wales. It has been suggested that he was trying to curry favour—he also named the distant hills Governor Darling Range. Face the river, then turn right and follow the path along to the next corner where you will be greeted by sweeping views across Melville Water, the widest part of the Swan River estuary.

The Narrows Bridge is below on the left, with the Kwinana Freeway snaking its traffic-filled way south along the edge of Melville Water. This broad stretch of the Swan River is filled with sails of all colours and sizes during summer weekends, and on weekday evenings when the river-based yacht clubs have their 'twilight sails'. Behind you is a rotunda erected in 1897, and a sundial memorial.

Keep following this path for about 300 metres, ignoring turns to the left and three sets of steps to the right. There are frequent glimpses of the red roof of the old Swan Brewery (see Walk 12) to the left. Natural bush covers the escarpment slopes, while the right side sees the beginning of the Botanic Park.

A gently sloping ramp leads off to the right. Follow this as it curves upward, to come alongside the Kimberley bed. This has a variety of plants from the far north Kimberley region of WA, including kapok

The Cenotaph, high on Anzac Bluff.

trees and bulbous boabs. Take the path right just before the last boab, into a large grassed area with a stone wall half concealing a car park.

Go left here across the lawn, which has superb views over Melville Water. Take the path leading off from the far corner, and ignore a turning to the left.

This leads into the Tuart Lawn, under the canopy of several grand old tuart trees. The Pioneer Women's Fountain is to the right, but for now, veer left towards the red tiled roof of another **Rotunda |5|**. The guns here were muzzle loading naval guns installed near the butts in 1905. They were buried in the sand when the butts were demolished and later brought here.

Take the path away from the river, at right angles to the path that brought you here. This leads down to the Water Garden, where several ponds and a stream are a re-creation of the predominantly granite land-scape of the Darling Range.

Turn left on the curving limestone path, past the middle pool with a set of sculp-tures which are a metaphor for Life. The pathway contains bronze plaques comme-morating various women's groups, and leads down to the Suffrage Memorial (following a bookleaf theme), which cele-brates the Centenary of Women's Suffrage here in WA. There's an unusual zinc-shingled pavilion across the lake, and a pair of tall karri trees with their shedding bark behind you. Their usual habitat is in the heavy rainfall areas of the south, where they grow to enormous heights.

Follow the path past the lake and then a sign marking the lower portion of the Acacia Garden. The paved path curves through beds of West Australian plants (many have identification labels) for several hundred metres. Look for the numerous banksias, zamias (an early form of palm) and grass-trees (formerly called blackboys). Grass-trees are strange shaggy plants with spiky grass-like leaves and long flowering stalks. They are also known as *Xanthor-roea*, or Balga. The bigger trees along here include jarrah, marri and she-oak.

The path winds upward and through a grove of melaleucas (paperbarks), then down to the Drummond Seat, commemo-rating the state's first botanist. Carry on past this and then take the first grass path to the right. As the area opens up there are three more boab trees on the right. These natives of the tropical northwest have recently been brought here—whether they will survive is a moot point. The area in front has several mottlecahs—long-limbed, straggly silver leafed eucalypts, which produce brilliant red blossoms in enormous gumnuts in early summer.

Proceed up to the circular stone **Roe Memorial |6|**, dedicated to Western Aus-tralia's first Surveyor-General. He was responsible for designing the layout of Perth, and for keeping what is now Kings Park in public hands. No one was allowed to own land here, though limestone could be quarried and jarrah logged. Strangely, the land was not gazetted until after he retired in 1871, when the first 432 acres were reserved. There's a splendid view over the Narrows Bridge and the city, which can be related to Roe's original plan engraved on the memorial.

Cross straight over the road behind the memorial, and follow the concrete strip road past the boom gate into part of the park's natural bushland, though there is little that matches the original vegetation of 1829. Sadly, this particular section has suffered from severe fires. Most of the big trees have gone, and mid-level plants seem to be taking over. Turn right at the first intersection. This track leads to a car park and the **DNA Observation Tower |7|**. Designed in the shape of the DNA double helix, the tower provides views to the hills and to the Indian Ocean. A direction chart is at the top.

Come back through the car park, down the left side of the drive, across the road, and down the dirt path back into the Botanic Gardens.

Take the first turn left and there is a big stand of Marri trees on the right. Marri is the Aboriginal word for blood, and the alternative English name is Red Gum, from the marri's habit of producing a red gum when damaged. Take the next turn right, around three paperbark trees, then left on to a grass path. This leads to the Acacia Steps, with lovely mosaics illustrating some of the acacia family. Note also the pod outlines carved into the rocks.

Turn left at the bottom of the steps, and go across the lawn to the lake with the **Pioneer Women's Memorial Fountain |8|**. Open air theatre is often presented here on summer evenings. Cross between the granite cascade and the lake, and follow the curved path up to the Banksia Garden. The curved seat has a banksia leaf design for its back support, while the five types found naturally in the park are shown in the stone floor.

Continue through the Banksia Garden, past a grand old grass-tree and the Aboriginal Scarred Tree (see notice). The next set of banksia seats has more mosaics. Turn left here down to the rock memorial which commemorates the establishment of the Botanic Garden, and go on to the Yorkas Nyinning, previously called Minmara Gun sculptured wall. This depicts females of all ages, and the name means 'Place where the Spirits of Women Rest'.

Turn right across the lawn, past the small circular building. The areas on either side have been dedicated to wildflowers, so are at their best late August to early October, and this is where the Wildflower Festival (held mid-September) has its base. Carry on to the road and turn right. Each of the roadside sugar gums is an individual living memorial to those who fell in two world wars, and this applies along the roads throughout the park. One quarter of the Anzacs at Gallipoli came from Western Australia, and over half the enlisted men in the First World War were casualties, either killed or discharged as medically unfit. This loss of manpower affected the state for a generation.

Just before the roundabout, on the left there's a single stunted oak, the last of the original memorial trees grown from acorns sent from Windsor Castle in the UK.

The statue in the middle of the roundabout is of **Lord John Forrest |9|**, the first Australian born peer, and a great influence upon the development of Western Australia. He was WA's first Premier, an architect of the Australian Federation, and one of the creators of Kings Park. Soon after Western Australia achieved self government in 1890, he increased the area of the park by another 550 acres, to almost its present size.

Continue over the roundabout to the Waterwise Garden. This is designed to encourage Perth residents to use local plants with low water requirements. The city has major water problems. All the possible dam sites throughout the Darling Range have been used, and close to the maximum amounts are already being drawn from ground water supplies. Perth has had below average rainfall for the last twenty years, and the water level in the dams has stayed below fifty percent of capacity, even at the end of the rainy season. Rationing is an ever constant threat.

Turn left past the garden, then cross back over the road to the enormous horizontal tree trunk, the **Karri Log |10|**, which came from the 'Big Tree' country of the southwest. Go past the log and information display area, and round the front of the café and visitor centre. Fraser's Restaurant is in front and a garden to the right. Go clockwise around the garden until you're in front of the Floral Clock.

Pass in front of the restaurant, along the grassy verge, to **Queen Victoria's statue |11|** surrounded by four cannons, and with cameo bronzes of Edward VII and his wife Alexandra. Continue across the grass to the old oriental style Tea Pavilion, built in 1898 and recently restored. Further on is another obelisk, the memorial to one of Western Australia's most famous cavalry regiments, the 10th Light Horse.

Turn left, away from the river, and follow the drive through a car park to the **Display Glasshouses |12|**. There are the Dry Inland, Kimberley, Fern and Pilbara Houses, with a Rare and Endangered Species Garden on the left hand side (see Opening Times). The research and nursery areas are behind the glasshouses. Kings Park is a world leader in its research into conservation ecology, particularly in the fields of cryo-storage and micro-propagation. On the way out note the 19th century saw pit opposite the entrance. This was how the felled trees were cut up, with one (unlucky) man in the pit and one above, using long saws.

Walk back over the lawns, beneath a collection of giant pine trees, probably planted in 1896, to Fraser Avenue, and turn left to the exit. This brings you back to the beginning of our walk.

Walk key

1. Barrack Square |
2. Riverside Drive |
3. Langley Park |
4. Heirisson Island |
5. Yagan |
6. McCallum Park |
7. Coode Street Jetty

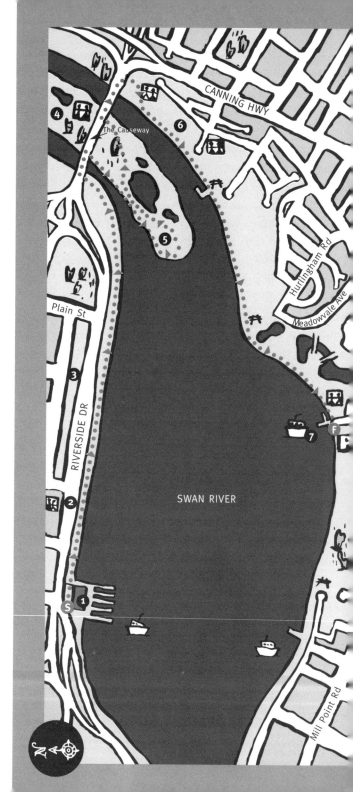

Perth Water
Perth's looking glass

Start

Barrack Square, Perth waterfront. This is the Blue CAT terminus. It's also easy walking distance from the city centre.

Finish

Coode Street Jetty, South Perth. Ferries to Barrack Square on weekdays September to April only or buses 102, 104 from Coode Street/Mill Point Road back to the city.

Length/Time

7 km/about 2 hours, ideally in the morning or evening.

Wheelchairs

Good access for wheelchair users, but bypass the rough terrain of Heirisson Island.

Perth Water, where the Swan River first broadens out, provides both a setting and a mirror for the city. It lies between Heirisson Island, an early hindrance to navigation, to the east, and The Narrows and Mt Eliza, with their strategic values, to the west. These features decided the location of Perth City.

Today the entire waterfront is accessible to the public, and much of it is parkland. Perth might not have great scenic beauty, but this stretch of water provides a beautiful and peaceful setting.

Barrack Square |1| was the old Perth Port, and now functions as the terminus for ferries and boat excursions. Simple ferries make frequent short trips across Perth Water to South Perth, while larger boats head off each morning down river and over to Rottnest. There are also excursions up river to the Swan Valley wine producing region, or down to Fremantle. The Western Australia Government and Perth City Council have grand ideas for the small garden area just behind the jetties. Further landscaping is planned, and a purpose built structure to house the eighteen bells of St Martin-in-the-Fields.

Oranges and lemons
Say the Bells of St Clement's
You owe me five farthings
Say the Bells of St Martin's ...

These are said to be the largest set of change-ringing bells in the world, and were given to Perth at the time of the Australian Bicentenary. A second stage of the redevelopment, channelling Riverside Drive through a tunnel, is mooted—to remove this major barrier between the city and the river.

Barrack Square is totally man-made. The original shoreline was 300 metres toward the city, at the line of the escarpment of skyscrapers, also known as the Great Wall. The banks were shallow and lined with reeds, and the settlers had to build jetties out into the river. Over the years these shallows were progressively filled in, with Barrack Square being created in 1903. It was also known as Union Jack or Flagstaff Square, because of its rectangular layout.

Today, in addition to the boat jetties, there are cafés with verandahs overlooking the river, souvenir shops, and a hire shop for boats and bikes, kayaks and fishing gear.

Facing the city, turn right along the river bank. The entire waterfront along **Riverside Drive |2|**, between Barrack Square and the Causeway, is being revamped to make it more attractive for people. There are limestone walkways and alcoves, lawns and gardens, benches and water fountains, and clumps of palm trees. Subtle floodlighting provides an appealing evening promenade. Various native flowers and shrubs, and palm trees (not native), have been planted in the median strip to improve the appearance. Even the volume of traffic should decrease with the opening of the Northbridge Tunnel (see Walk 5) as an alternative route to Riverside Drive.

The refurbished boatshed on the right is the home of the Western Australia Rowing Club, and has a small café. Beyond, there are clear views across Perth Water to South Perth (see Walk 11). A line of timber posts in the river marks the limit of a dredged channel and provides good resting points for the numerous cormorants. The channel enables boats to sail upstream. Perth Water is remarkably shallow and, in its natural state, could be waded across. This makes it ideal for safe novice sailing, and explains the presence of dozens of small yachts (surfcats) on the water during the warmer months.

To the left, across Riverside Drive, you can see the tree lined Supreme Court

Gardens (see Walk 1), a favourite summer venue for open-air concerts, especially during the Perth International Arts Festival. The gardens give way to a large barren car park, with Government House and Perth Concert Hall behind.

Past Victoria Avenue, the open grassed area to the left is **Langley Park |3|**, Perth's first official airfield from 1921, when it became a base for Western Australian Airways. One of their early pilots was Charles Kingsford Smith, who subsequently went on to set many long distance flying records in 'Southern Cross'. The park, edged with coral trees, is now occasional home to light aircraft, sporting teams and rally cars when it's the base for the Australian leg of the world rallying championship. Roads, ramps and bridges, and swathes of grandstands appear almost overnight, the park reverberates to the roar of revving engines, and then goes back to its usual sleepy, and rather plain, existence.

Just behind the park is a line of apartment buildings, and the back entrance to the ABC Studios. This is a lower version of the Great Wall and, as before, marks the original shoreline.

An enormous area of shallows was filled in, to create this belt of rather boring parkland, and the straight line of the waterfront. One major advantage is that the riverfront has been left uncluttered by buildings and open to public use. The building of Riverside Drive was a relief measure during the Great Depression of the 1930s. Langley Park extends quite a

Opening Times
Surfcat hire: October–May, 9am–sunset.

Refreshments
Cafés at start and finish, little between. A few drinking fountains.

long way (which befits an airfield) and so does your path.

Continue past the Plain Street traffic lights, to where Riverside Drive curves away to the left. The path continues past a stand of needle-leafed casuarinas. The wind makes a lovely sound blowing through these trees. **Heirisson Island |4|**, visited later in the walk, appears across a narrowing stretch of river. Over to the left are the enormous concrete light towers of the WACA cricket ground (see Walk 9), with the curved front of the Police Headquarters in front. Go past the fenced enclosure used for helicopter trips along the river. These operate on Saturdays and Sundays from September to April, weather permitting.

The path curves left past a car park, and a bike and kayak hire outlet, towards the bridge. Go left at the fork, up to the road, and cross the first span of the Causeway over to Heirisson Island. The path across the bridge is right next to the road, with six lanes of constant traffic thundering past. Go right immediately after the bridge and walk along the path by the river, but now going downstream.

This point was the early limit of naviga-tion up the Swan River—there were mud flats and reed beds surrounding several low-lying islands. Both Dutch (1697) and French (1801) explorers sailed up to this point, and the Heirisson Islands took their name from the leader of the French party that came up river.

The entire Swan Valley is the context for the Aboriginal dreaming story about the

Statue of Yagan, on Heirisson Island.

waugyl (a spiritual watersnake), and one version of the story tells that at this point the waugyl shook itself, flinging off numerous scales which formed these islands.

Even James Stirling, who founded the colony of Western Australia, thought that this was the Swan River delta, and gave the name Melville Water to the entire stretch of river below here, as though it was an arm of the sea. The islands were a major hindrance to navigation, and a canal was cut to get around the problem (see Walk 10). This had limited success, and later the islands were consolidated into one and channels dredged in the river.

Go through the fence at the double gates. Please note the warnings about kangaroos which have been settled on this part of the island. They tend to rest in the shade during the hottest time of the day, so might not be seen.

Continue along the shoreline, with trees, mostly casuarinas, partially concealing the emerging view of the city centre. Near the tip of the island, turn left up a small grassed knoll to a bronze statue.

This is **Yagan |5|**, who was a leader of Aboriginal people from the upper Swan area at the time of settlement. At first there were good relations between the Aboriginals and settlers, but the vast differences between their cultures and concepts of ownership soon caused misunderstandings which led to conflict. Yagan tried for reconciliation but a series of disputes and killings destroyed this hope. He was captured once and exiled to Carnac Island (near Rottnest), but outwitted his captors and escaped in their boat. He was later outlawed and then shot and decapitated. His smoke-dried head was sent to the UK, and has only recently been reclaimed. His statue has been decapitated twice, but statues can have new heads welded on.

Go down the opposite slope, behind Yagan, and then left to follow the near shoreline of two small lakes. This is one of those city spots which could be miles from anywhere. On reaching the kangaroo fence go to another set of gates to the right, pass through them, then follow the cream gravel track back towards the bridge. Cross through the railings and turn right over the second bridge span. There's a good view on

the left towards Burswood Casino Resort. Once across the bridge take the first fork right (labelled to South Perth), then left at the water's edge. Note that there are separate paths here for pedestrians and cyclists.

This stretch of water, with Heirisson Island beyond, is used for water-skiing in summer. **McCallum Park |6|** is on the left, with several public tennis courts. The path winds along the shoreline, past clumps of trees. It circles a group of fenced off buildings and a jetty, belonging to the Fisheries Department, past a small car park and along more parkland, with houses beyond. You can see the end of Heirisson Island and the traffic along Riverside Drive.

Further on there's another small car park, with nearby barbecues and picnic shelters. There are two artificial bird-littered lakes off to the left, on what was once the Kensington Park Race Course.

Finally, there are several buildings and car parks, where Coode Street runs down to the foreshore. Go around the first building, Wesley College Rowing Club, to the Boatshed Café, a splendid spot for refreshments with a view. The **Coode Street Jetty |7|** is in front of it. Just beyond is the surfcat hire facility, which operates from October to May. The river is shallow and safe and messing about in boats can be a good way to spend a quiet hour on the water.

The walk ends here. If the Coode Street ferry isn't running, the Mends Street service is another kilometre along the shore, or there are buses near the Coode Street/Mill Point Road intersection.

Walk key

1. Queen's Gardens | 2. WACA | 3. East Perth Cemetery | 4. Waterloo Crescent |
5. Claisebrook Inlet | 6. Claisebrook Cove | 7. Originating fountain | 8. Boans Furniture
Factory | 9. Mardalup Park | 10. Trafalgar Road footbridge | 11. Victoria Gardens

East Perth

Old meets new...

Start

Queen's Gardens, corner Hay/Plain streets.
Take Red CAT to Queen's Gardens stop, or any bus travelling east along Adelaide Terrace (to Plain Street).

Finish

Corner Trafalgar/Royal streets, East Perth.
Take the Red CAT, or buses 91, 92, 95 back to the city.

Length/Time

4.4 km/2.5 hours
(longer if taking WACA tour, or visiting the cemetery).

Wheelchairs

Generally good access for wheelchair users. Some moderately steep slopes.

East Perth is tucked within a curve of the Swan River, where Claisebrook flows into it, upstream from Perth Water.

For years it was out of sight, and mind. Claisebrook was polluted, and the surrounding industries had become obsolete and derelict.

A major urban renewal project has transformed the stream, streets and structures to create an attractive new residential area, with Claisebrook as the focus. Public artworks, water features, numerous pedestrian pathways, and a recognition of the Aboriginal heritage add to the ambience.

Closer to the Causeway are Perth's major sporting venues for cricket and trotting. There's also the East Perth Cemetery, Perth's original burial ground, and Queen's Gardens whose clay made the bricks for most of the city's early buildings.

Enter **Queen's Gardens** |1| through the wrought iron gates bearing the City of Perth coat of arms, appropriately showing the black swan. There may be a sign in summer saying 'Please close the gates for the safety of our cygnets'. The park is a quiet, well-maintained haven with a series of small lakes, where clay pits once operated. The lovely old multi-hued bricks used in many of Perth's 19th century buildings (see Walk 1) were made here, until the Government took over the site in 1899.

Cross diagonally over the lawn towards the tall light towers beyond, as far as the Peter Pan statue. This delightful piece, with Peter Pan on high and people and creatures emerging from the swirling base, is a replica of the Kensington Gardens original. The base is signed, not by the sculptor but by the author, J.M.Barrie. Continue on, crossing a pair of small bridges, to the far corner where storerooms are sheltered by a giant Moreton Bay fig, and a gate leads out on to Nelson Crescent.

Leave the gardens and turn right to cross the road to the West Australian Cricket Association ground, known universally as the **WACA** |2|. The soaring concrete light towers enable games to be played at night (cricket in summer and various forms of football in winter), and are visible from many parts of the city.

Go straight ahead, along Nelson Street, to Gate 2 of the WACA. You may be allowed to enter and look at the ground, if there is no match being played. Tours of the ground and the cricket museum are availa-ble as shown opposite in Opening Times. This area was first set aside as Perth Meadows for general recreation, but then in 1899, 14 acres were vested in the WACA, and it has grown progressively to be acknowledged now as one of the most attractive test match venues in the world.

The large, ornate curved gateway across the road leads into the Gloucester Park Raceway, home of the Western Australia Trotting Association. The gates were the winning design of a competition when the track was developed in 1929, and look like the ceremonial entry to some great Empire stadium. Cross over to the gates and go back along Nelson, before taking the first turn right up Hale Street, then right again into Waterloo Crescent. Nelson and Water-loo are the only curved streets (going around a small hill here) in central Perth (excluding Horseshoe Bridge). The view from the houses on the left is rather spoilt by the high brick wall around Gloucester Park—which stops people having free views (and falls down the steep slope).

Go around the curve to where Bronte Street enters from the left. Beyond it are the grounds of the **East Perth Cemetery** |3|, enclosing St Bartholomew's Chapel, sitting on top of the highest land in central Perth below Kings Park. Both cemetery and chapel are listed on the Register of the National Estate. Cemetery Hill was set aside in 1829 as the burial ground for Perth, and it remained such until 1899, by which date the growing city had reached here—and people don't like living next to a cemetery. There were actually seven cemeteries here based on denomination, and including Chinese. The Church of England part was the most important, and is where St Bartholomew's is located. This lovely little church was the mortuary chapel before becoming a parish church, until 1970. It was designed by the Colonial Architect Richard Roach Jewell, who was later buried here, and there are several later additions. If it's not possible to visit the cemetery, disregard the next three paragraphs, and continue the walk from Waterloo Crescent.

On Sunday afternoons only, turn left here to the gate leading into the cemetery and through into the chapel. The interior is quite simple, though there's a mural curtained off behind the altar—(it was deemed unsuitable for public display). The she-oak shingle roof was replaced in 1998, and is one of the few such roofs exposed and still functional in the city.

There are a few gravestones worth looking at. Coming out of the chapel, immediately on the right, there's a tall pointed iron memorial to three explorers killed in the northwest (they have another memorial in Fremantle—see Walk 17). Next to this is the family plot for Walter Padbury, an important merchant. A little further away from the chapel, under trees, is a group of three headstones within railings, telling the sad tale of Richard Jones who passed away in 1876, but whose wife Louisa had died (presumably in childbirth) way back in 1830, and then the surviving child three months later.

Opening Times

WACA Museum and Ground Tours:
October 1–March 31, Tues and Thurs (other months Tues only) 10am, unless a match is being played.
East Perth Cemetery and St Bartholomew's Church:
Sun 2pm–4pm (small fee).

Refreshments

Several drinking fountains. Cafés planned for redevelopment area.

Come back out of the cemetery gates and turn left, to rejoin the walk at the corner of Waterloo Crescent and Bronte Street.

Walk along **Waterloo Crescent |4|**, (the continuation point if you bypassed the cemetery), beside the cemetery fence, until the fence curves away. Most of the grave stones in this area are from the 1890s when Perth's population was expanding (and dying) with the Gold Rush. Turn right into Nile Street, towards the river. On the left is some of the new housing in the East Perth Redevelopment Area, though some old houses have survived. Across the road the Gloucester Park great wall actually stops, allowing unimpeded views of the track.

Where Nile Street curves right, below Gloucester Park, cross over to go left along the Swan River path. More of the new housing is on the left with great views across the river. The redevelopment is transforming what was a degraded and deteriorating industrial landscape into commercial properties and lively, medium density upmarket housing areas.

Continue along the path, past a Peace Grove dedicated to President Sadat and Premier Rabin, then curving round a retaining wall sheltering a stone settee and Deborah's Chair. Turn right onto a small headland, and follow the trail which winds around a group of twelve tall boulders. This area has had human significance for probably thousands of years. Nearby wetlands and springs, and the Swan River, provided consistent food supplies for the local Aboriginal people.

Peter Pan statue in Queen's Gardens.

One of the major features of Perth when first settled was a string of shallow lakes lying immediately to the north of the city. One was Tea Tree Lake on Clause's Brook, which drained into the Swan River just above here. These lakes were subsequently emptied through a drain into renamed Claisebrook, which became ugly and polluted. It received effluent from a tannery, soap factory, four saw mills, brickworks, stables, laundries and foundries. The twelve boulders represent twelve lakes which disappeared beneath modern Perth, set along a dreaming track winding along the edge of a rejuvenated **Claisebrook Inlet** |5|. The inlet is another feature of the redevelopment, as is the series of public artworks that line its shores. Just by the last of the boulders are two lovely old pieces of tree trunk, rubbed smooth over years of touching. This is Yoondoorup Boorna, the Claisebrook Tree.

Go along the inlet shore, in the lee of a high retaining wall, to where some sombre sculpted panels appear within a semi-classical setting. It's rather strange, though attractive. Continue, passing beneath the small suspension bridge, to where the inlet widens out to become **Claisebrook Cove** |6|. A hotel, tavern and waterside cafés are all planned to be open on the left by 2001. The opposite shore is entirely residential, behind the tall stilted sculpture standing in the water. The Cove has several timber posts and curved seats, made from local salvage materials. Two have stylised shipping channel markers on top.

Walk along the boardwalks to the top of the Cove, to pass through the tunnel there. The stream trickles along a small channel decorated with stone turtles. The tunnel walls have a series of phrases giving word pictures of East Perth's history.

Through the tunnel there's a turtle-stepped lake with a bubbling brown fountain. Eastbrook Village is on the left, and commercial properties can be seen beyond the lawns on the right. Carry on around the lake and along the trickling brook, around Regency Crescent

to another stream-lined tunnel, this one decorated with definitions of local words, both English and Aboriginal.

Keep following the pathway, past the Firewall Fountain made from locally produced bricks, to the **originating fountain** |7| where the water is pushing its way through fractured rocks. Across the path is a drinking fountain with some evocative inscriptions.

This is where the redevelopment area meets the outside world. Just over Fielder Street, on the right, is the Advanced Manufacturing Technologies Centre—the nano-centre of Western Australia's attempt to develop industries for the 21st century. Half hidden behind the trees opposite the AMTC is 'Silver City' (named for its aluminium cladding), home of the Education Department of Western Australia. Further to the left is a small brick building which was part of the East Perth School. Where practical, heritage buildings have been retained as part of the redevelopment, and the school is one of them.

Turn right into Fielder Street, then right again after ten metres, on to a footpath which leads into Saunders Street. Go past the car park and over some grass to a tall thin statue. **Boans Furniture Factory** |8| just to the left is another refurbished heritage building. Boans was Perth's major department store (since taken over by Myers), built in Wellington Street (see Walk 2) on the site of one of the lakes that coincidentally was drained through Claisebrook. The factory has been adapted for studio apartments.

Go straight on to join the footpath of the street curving in from the right. The roundabout ahead in Claisebrook Square has another piece of public art—a large, angular sculpture made of textured aluminium. It's based on Penrose's *'Impossible Triangle'*, which is an optical illusion of a triangle where the sides connect in an apparently impossible way. The view of the sculpture varies as one goes around it.

Cross the road to the right, before the roundabout. This is the 'privileged position' where the arms of the sculpture meet to complete the triangle. Proceed down the steps or ramp to the small Eastbrook Lake, which you came past earlier in the walk. Go left to cross the bridge and back through the tunnel to Claisebrook Cove.

Cross the next small bridge to go along the left hand side of the cove, past the standing figure and boat sculpture, made from recycled jarrah and old boat parts. The 'head' acts as a wind vane. The impressive town houses here open onto Henry Lawson Walk. The great Australian writer came to Perth at the height of the Gold Rush in 1896, on his honeymoon! There was literally no room at the inn, so the first night was under the Barrack Street Bridge (see Walk 5), and they then stayed in the Government Camp, a tent city next to Claisebrook.

'We have given up the awful hunt for lodgings, and have joined a camp by the river ... and are now the proud possessor of a bag-and-canvas-covered frame, with a tent inside. Our Government camp is on a sandy slope, with the cemetery on the

ridge, and an alleged stream—called officially "the Brook"—along the bottom of the slope. We found, soon enough, that the brook was one of the city's natural sewers—perhaps the main one.'

Pass back under the suspension bridge, and curve around the triangular boat entry markers and moorings. There's a better view of the large mural, and its setting, across the inlet. It's much clearer, better proportioned and more appealing from here. Carry on down to the edge of the Swan River. There are splendid views up and down stream and across to Burswood Park and Resort.

Go left along the bank, and turn left where the path curves away from the river, towards the squat grey sculpture. Go to the right of this concentric creation and follow the grey curving line, with stream-of-consciousness words embedded in it. This was the site of the East Perth Gasworks, yet another industry that developed here. There is a line of timber marker posts curving away across what is now called **Mardalup Park |9|**. These mark the original shoreline, and carry pictures, diagrams, definitions and quotes relating to the gasworks. Over beyond the markers are the railway bridge and embankment (see Walk 10), and behind that the towering remains of the East Perth Power Station. Much of this is to be retained, though its future use is uncertain.

Turn away from the river and go up the small paved street, past more modern mansions. Turn left into Henry Lawson

Walk, and go around the new head office for Heytesbury Holdings, the company run by Janet (widow of entrepreneur, Robert) Holmes á Court. This houses both a restaurant and the Holmes á Court Gallery, whose prime purpose will be to provide a home for one of the most extensive art collections in the country. Stay at the upper level, to cross the **Trafalgar Road footbridge |10|**, with great views over the Cove to the city skyline. On the other side, bear left over the grass to the red and white roofed pavilion which houses a marble sarcophagus commemorating the old park that was once here and its little caretaker's cottage. The park is now called **Victoria Gardens |11|**.

Continue past the pavilion to the fortress-like structure beyond, with good views over the river. The floor has a wonderful coloured mosaic of the Charnock Woman, incorporating Aboriginal, Celtic and white Australian themes. A plaque on the wall gives some of the mythology of the Bibbulmun nation, including references to the magpies and stars that are features of the mosaic. The slots in the fortress walls mark the direction of sunrise at different times of the year.

Cross back over the park, passing left of the pavilion, to a ring of six stones, representing the leaders of the local Aboriginal communities at the time of white settlement. Continue to the path under the two giant pines, and turn left to the corner of Trafalgar Road and Royal Street. The walk ends here, and bus stops are a few metres away.

Walk key

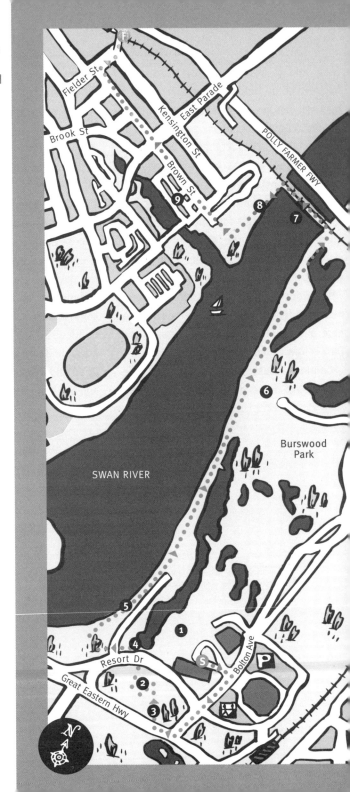

Burswood

From rubbish dump to casino

Start

Burswood Resort Casino.
Take the train to Burswood
Railway Station (Armadale
line); any of buses 36,
200–202, 208, 209, 285, 287,
298, 300, 302; or the Perth
Tram to the Burswood
Casino stop.

Finish

Claisebrook Station, East Perth.
Catch the train (Armadale Line)
or bus 82 in East Parade,
to central Perth.

Length/Time

5.3 km/2 hours

Wheelchairs

Good conditions for
wheelchair users. The railway
bridge has a ramp.

Burswood is located just across the
Swan River from East Perth, and has
played a significant if low-key role in
Perth's history. Early explorers and
settlers came upriver by boat, but
were prevented from proceeding
beyond this point by mudflats, though
a canal provided some relief. Burswood
became a dairy farm, but for many years
this century, it was a rubbish tip and
an eyesore.

Since 1980 the transformation has
been quite amazing. The casino, hotel,
dome and convention centre are major
attractions, but most of the area is
splendidly restored public land, the
Burswood Park. A significant feature is
the Heritage Trail, with bronze statues
reflecting Western Australia's history.
The walk explores Burswood before
crossing the Swan River, and finishing
in East Perth.

The casino is the only casino licensed to operate in Western Australia, and attracts many tourists, especially highrollers to its elite International Gaming Room.

Immediately adjacent is the five star **Burswood Resort Hotel |1|**, with superb views over to the city across the Swan River. A significant feature is the enormous, palm-lined, full-height, glass atrium. The Burswood Convention Centre and Showroom, with its stepped frontage, is the next building to the right.

Take the covered footpath to the right (away from the hotel), past the stairs leading to the undercroft car park, and follow the curve around to the right. The Burswood Dome, with its curved 'roof', is directly in front of you. This is claimed to be the largest enclosed stadium in Australia. A feature of the dome is its unobstructed viewing, due to the column-free, inflated roof which is held aloft by eight huge fans maintaining a constant air pressure.

Continue along the path, next to a dual carriageway, past palm trees, lawns and flower beds. At the roundabout, carry on in the same direction down to the traffic lights at the major intersection ahead. This is the Great Eastern Highway, the main gateway to the city for visitors from the airport, Kalgoorlie and the Eastern States.

The path veers right just before the highway to become a multi-use path. This section of the walk runs parallel with the highway, with extensive garden beds, lawns and trees on both sides of the road. The **Citizen of the Year Lake |2|** appears

ahead, with a brick path leading off to the right. Follow this path around some bushes to a large bronze statue. This is the start of the **Heritage Trail |3|**, a representation in bronze of some of the figures and events of Western Australia's history. The trail is the concept and work of two Irish sculptors, Joan Walsh-Smith and Charles Smith, who settled here in 1985, looking for adventure and opportunity. Each statue has its own setting and descriptive plaque, telling its story of Perth and Western Australia. They're all lifelike, involved in distinctive and real activities, and they're all placed at ground level, rather than on pedestals. This gives them a quite particular relevance and attraction, and it's not unusual to see children crawling all over them.

After studying Henry Camfield, forever wiping the sweat from his brow, go back along the brick path towards the highway, and across the dual use path. Note the moulded paving stones set into the brick path, with motifs of local plant life. The next statue is that of Paddy Hannan whose discovery of gold at Kalgoorlie in 1893 transformed Western Australia. He is shown glancing away to his right, watching today's constant flow of traffic along the highway heading off towards his Kalgoorlie.

Follow the winding Heritage Trail and turn off to the white Swan Shell, a graceful, soaring Concord-like structure, poised ready for take-off. On summer weekends, the Shell may be used by wedding groups or open air performers. Go across, or round the front of, the Shell and down another brick path, which curves to the right through a small group of gum trees. An opening in the garden beds on the right hand side leads down to a paved area in front of Citizen of the Year Lake.

The glorious statue rising out of it is arguably Western Australia's finest—the Swan Fountain. Five giant swans, one above the other, leap skywards among a cascade of water jets, with spray sparkling in the sunlight. Truly superb, it looks great in any light, but especially in the early morning or late evening. This is also the work of Joan and Charles Smith, for whom the challenge was to capture the soul and spirit of the place, and to produce an ongoing symbol. 'We'd gone down to the lake to get the feel of the place, and were sitting there, when two swans just flew in and landed on the water, so the statue designed itself.'

The symbol of the swan is used for the annual Citizen of the Year awards, and set around this small paved area are the names of the recipients.

Go back to the path and turn right, towards the hotel and casino, and continue left where the path splits. Cross the road (Resort Drive), and the low building in front is the Tourism Council's **Visitor Information Centre |4|**. It is worth going in here to view the displays and to collect some brochures about the park. A particularly useful one is *Birds of Burswood Park.*

Return to the road and follow the sidewalk to the right, away from the hotel. Cross the next road (Camfield Drive), and

Opening Times
Casino: open 24 hours every day of the week.

Refreshments
Casino and hotel at the beginning. Water fountains and occasional ice cream van in Burswood Park. Lunch bars near the end (from Mon—Fri only).

continue to the brick path, which is the Heritage Trail again, and turn right. To the left is a picnic area, while on the right is the next statue, *'Hopscotch: Children at Play'*. The rules are given on the reverse side of the explanatory sign, and there are two outlines laid out for children (or others) to play the game themselves. Just beyond is a modern, bright scarlet and yellow, children's playground, and then on the left is the last water fountain followed *by The Storyteller.* This statue is based on the person and the stories of Dame Mary Durack, one of Australia's foremost historical novelists. She is shown reading her *Swan River Saga* to a small girl—actually a representation of Mary herself as a child.

The brick path now forms a T-junction with another dual use path. Cross this to stand on the grassy bank of the Swan River. To the left is part of the Causeway bridge, which leads into the City of Perth, and directly in front is Heirisson Island (see Walk 8). Beyond the island is another channel of the Swan River and then the tall light towers of the WACA (West Australian Cricket Association ground), while the stadium to its right is the Gloucester Park trotting ground (see Walk 9).

Follow the dual use path upstream, away from the Causeway, to the next set of statues, a man and a swan facing each other in incredulous amazement. They represent **Willem de Vlamingh |5|** and his first sighting of the exotic black swan. Vlamingh is significant in that he explored and charted much of our west coast over three hundred years ago, and sailed up the river he called the *Swartte Swaane Drift* (Black Swan current or stream). He was able to travel upstream only as far as this part of the river, a series of mudflats and reedbeds here and around nearby Heirisson Island preventing further navigation.

A little way beyond Vlamingh a plaque has been erected to commemorate the victory of Shirley Taylor-Smith in the 25 kilometre World Championship swim in 1991. To the right is a good view of the five star Burswood Hotel jutting out to provide panoramic views of the river and city for its guests. This is the end of the Heritage Trail, though other statues are planned.

The rest of the walk along this side of the river is extremely pleasant and restful. The change from just a few years ago is quite amazing, because for forty years this whole area—casino, heritage trail and all—was the Rivervale Dump. A sodden, rotten mass

Swan Fountain along the Burswood Heritage Trail.

of garbage, cinders, car bodies, bitumen and rubble. The Burswood Park Board was only established in 1986, and transforming this horror was its main challenge. Burswood Park is no longer a degraded site, but has won its category of the Western Australia Tourism awards three years in a row, and is now in the Tourism Hall of Fame.

The dual use path curves around the Burswood Water Sports Centre, a major speedboat and water-skiing venue. These users have a long term lease dating from rubbish tip time, so the river is not always as restful as it might be, especially over summer weekends.

A long, curving fountain-festooned lake separates the path from the hotel and convention centre and then the start of Burswood Park Public Golf Course. There are occasional plaques on the grassy banks giving information on the various bird species that are commonly found here. Black swans, cormorants, ducks and coots are seen, and one of the regular delights is the sight of pelicans soaring around the park and river.

Beyond the lake, there is a high fence to separate golfers (and golf balls) from walkers. The path passes a series of large, spreading fig trees, which provide shady viewing points close to the **Golf Clubhouse** |6|. About two hundred metres further along and directly across the river is the inlet of Claisebrook (see Walk 9), with its small suspension bridge framing the towers of central Perth.

The path continues along the river as far as the **Goongoongup Railway Bridge** |7|, where it curves around and up to a recessed walk/cycle way set into the side of the bridge. The walk follows this route, with pleasing views downstream to the Burswood complex. Coming off the bridge, follow the curving path left and back down to the river's edge. Turn right at the bottom and then fork right to pass in front of the first houses. The path goes between three strange **industrial artworks** |8|—the right-

hand one is called *Steel Magnolias*—inspired by and created from the old gasworks which sat on the river bank here. This is the **East Perth Redevelopment Area** |9|, where a derelict industrial landscape is being transformed into a mostly residential suburb (see Walk 9). Follow the path as it curves across parkland, between a series of timber mooring posts. Each of these carries information about the old gasworks.

At the end of the path, immediately after the basketball court, turn right up Brown Street. Continue along Brown Street past Henry Lawson Walk which leads down to the suspension bridge over Claisebrook Cove (see Walk 9). There is housing on the left hand side of the road, and an interesting commercial development on the right. Old commercial properties have been converted and given a new front featuring painted arches and rural views.

The next major intersection is East Parade, with the No. 82 bus stop twenty metres to the right. Cross East Parade, and follow Brown Street along a rather run down, low-key commercial streetscape. There are two lunch bars in the street, only open on weekdays.

The end of Brown Street is a T-junction with Fielder Street, with the modern architecture of the Advanced Manufacturing Technologies Centre across the road. Turn right here, to the pedestrian bridge which leads over the railway tracks to Claisebrook Station. The walk ends here.

Walk key

1. Mends Street Jetty |
2. Shenton's Mill | 3. Police Station | 4. Perth Zoo |
5. Old Mill Theatre |
6. Windsor Hotel |
7. Sir James Mitchell Park |
8. Stand of paperbarks

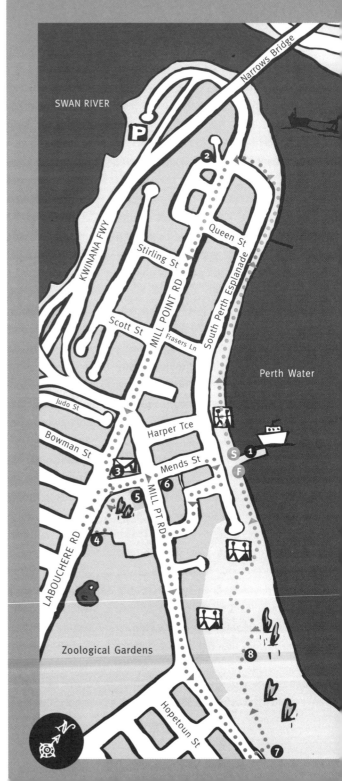

South Perth

Across Perth Water: view and zoo!

Start

Mends Street Jetty, South Perth. Ferries from Barrack Square Jetty, close to the city centre.

Finish

The starting point with regular ferries back to Barrack Street jetty.

Length/Time

4.6 km/about 2 hours

Wheelchairs

Generally good access for wheelchair users, but entry to Sir James Mitchell Park will require a diversion—continue about 150 metres further along Mill Point Road.

South Perth has long been a major suburb, with its proximity to the city, and with river frontages on two sides.

The area was part of the original Perth townsite, and had one of the first industries: Shenton's Mill, at Point Belches which is now known as The Narrows. For many years it was a quiet, peaceful and remote (the only access was via the Causeway) suburb, but that changed with the opening of the Narrows Bridge and the Kwinana Freeway. The sleepy backwater was transformed, with most of the grand old waterfront houses replaced by blocks of apartments, especially on the high ground once known as Yellow Hill.

Occasional gems still exist, including Shenton's Mill. South Perth is also home to the Perth Zoo.

The first **Mends Street Jetty** |1| was built in 1894 to run paddle-steamers, and a ferry service has operated to the city ever since.

Turn right along the dedicated pedestrian path just beyond the jetty, crossing the parkland towards the Narrows Bridge. You are parallel with the South Perth Esplanade which has been a prime address for many years, offering superb views to the city.

Only a few private houses are left among the apartment blocks, but they show a great variety of styles. No. 69 is a large mock Tudor hidden behind a great wall, on the corner of Harper Terrace. No. 39, Haddon Place, is a massive balconied development, which replaced a delightful Victorian mansion called Haddon Hall. A gracious, curved modernist house at No. 27 is half hidden by a row of cypresses, while there is a Dutch barn style house at No. 23.

Continue past the small Queen Street Jetty, round the bend where there are great views of the Narrows Bridge and Kings Park behind, with the Cenotaph standing out at the summit of Anzac Bluff (see Walk 7). You can also see the stepped line of buildings down the slope of Mount Street, from Kings Park, to the city highrises.

At the end of the buildings along The Esplanade there is an open area before the Narrows Bridge. This was originally a small inlet, Miller's Bay, which provided easy water access to **Shenton's Mill** |2|. Cut across here to the left, between the houses and the trees, towards the mill half hidden next to a tall Norfolk Island pine. Go down the left side to the wooden lichgate entrance. Entry is $2.00 (free to National Trust members). Both mill and cottage date from 1835 (the 1833 mill burnt down) though major renovation was necessary in both 1929 and 1958. There are interesting displays and a collection of carriages and buggies, somewhat incongruous with the freeway traffic roaring past just the other side of the fence.

On leaving, turn left and then proceed to the right along Mill Point Road, South Perth's main street. This area is a peninsula jutting out into the river (and creating The Narrows), so there are views to the City, Kings Park and over Melville Water. Mill Point Road, like The Esplanade, is full of apartment blocks, and No. 34 (Twin Waters, on the corner of Queen Street), with its enormous plant-filled balconies on all sides, illustrates the advantages of the location.

Continue along this shaded, leafy street to the traffic lights, where you cross straight over into Labouchere Road (Mill Point Road goes left). At the first corner, with Mends Street, is the 1909 **Police Station** |3|. With its brick and stucco frontage it looks just like a typical charming cottage of the period.

Carry on across Mends Street, noting the pleasant weatherboard cottage at No. 35, as far as the entrance to **Perth Zoo** |4| under its peaked canvas awnings. It opened in 1898, and helped define South Perth as a desirable suburb. The Zoo has changed considerably over the years to maintain its appeal and relevance, with its animal enclosures redesigned to closely replicate the natural wildlife habitats. It's now one of a worldwide group concentrating on the preservation and breeding of certain endangered species.

Return to Labouchere Road and turn right back into Mends Street, round the greens of the South Perth Bowling Club to the **Old Mill Theatre |5|**. This was originally the Mechanics Institute, but now houses one of the oldest and most successful of Perth's community theatre groups. Continue past the wooden water trough and round the corner of a lovely red bricked, tuck pointed building, the South Perth Heritage House. This was originally the Council Offices, but is now a historical and theatrical museum.

Come back to the corner. Across the road, the low iron-roofed building is the South Perth Post Office dating from 1900, and on your right the restored **Windsor Hotel |6|**. Cross over and go in the front door (ten metres to the right along Mill Point Road). The lobby has some good decorative plasterwork and superb leadlight windows. The first door on the right leads into the Duchess Room, which was modelled after one of the first South Perth ferries *The Duchess*, with its curved timber ceiling and historic river photographs. The upstairs portion of the hotel is under repair, but the balconies should be open again in late 1999.

Turn right out of the hotel and immediately right down Mends Street, through the main shopping centre. There are still a few old buildings—low single stories with bullnose verandahs—such as Nos. 11 to 15 across the road. Carry on down to the

Opening Times

Shenton's Mill: daily 10am–4pm (not public holidays).
Perth Zoo: daily 9am–5pm.
South Perth Heritage House: Mon, Wed, Thurs 1pm–5pm; Sat 9am–12 noon.

Refreshments

Hotel, shops and cafés in Mends Street, and at the Zoo.

bottom, around Coco's Bar/Restaurant to the right, and then right after Shoppers' Car Park, up the unnamed no-entry street. Follow the footpath, up and to the left, and then right at the next street to come back to Mill Point Road. Turn left here, with the zoo off to the right behind a line of tall Moreton Bay Figs. On the left is a series of even taller apartment blocks, all with stunning views over the Swan River to the city and beyond. There is an occasional glimpse between the buildings. It's hard to imagine that this was Tom Hungerford's sleepy Suburban Road (*Tales from a Suburban Road*), written in the 1930s, before both name and character changed.

Over the brow of the hill and round the bend there's a sudden and glorious change, as the highrises give way to a broad green sweep of parkland running all the way to the river.

Burswood Resort and the light towers of the WACA can be seen across the river, to the right of the city proper. **Sir James Mitchell Park |7|** (named after a former Premier and Governor of Western Australia) is a glorious stretch of public open space, where once were market gardens. The Gold Rush of the 1880s and 1890s brought many Chinese to Western Australia, and some of them leased this land to produce perhaps Perth's finest vegetables. Go along to, and down, the stone-lined steps. Across the park to the right you can see a fleet of masts, where small catamarans can be hired for sailing around Perth Water. This is a great way to spend an idle hour.

Shenton's Mill, dating from 1835.

The walk continues left along the sealed path from the foot of the steps, for about two hundred metres. Cut right across the grass, just after the palm tree, to a thick grove of trees.

A winding wooden boardwalk leads through this **stand of paperbarks |8|**, and over a small wetland. Ducks and songbirds, shade and dappled light, peace and quiet and wooden benches make this a truly delightful spot. At the end of the boardwalk, go half left towards a wooden archway which leads into a small enclosed garden with drinking fountains and more birds—and more peace.

Come back out and follow the brick path towards the Swan River. Cross the sealed multi-use path, watching out for cyclists, rollerbladers, joggers, and people exercising their dogs. There are picnic tables and free barbecue facilities to the right, but the walk goes left along the river bank. The highrises, to the left, seem somehow remote on the slopes of what was once sand, giving the old nickname of Yellow Hill. This is one of the best spots to appreciate the layout of the city—across Perth Water. The reflections can be wonderful, especially at sunset.

The walk finishes back at the Mends Street Jetty.

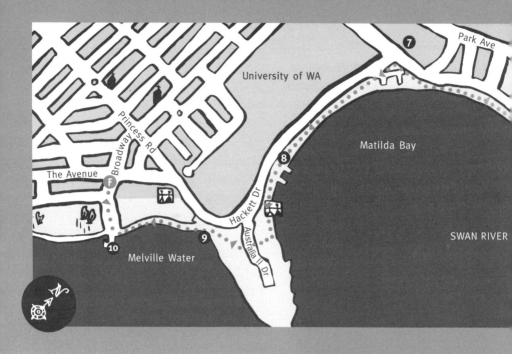

University of WA

Park Ave

Matilda Bay

Princess Rd

Broadway

The Avenue

Hackett Dr

Australia II Dr

SWAN RIVER

Melville Water

Walk key

1. Barrack Square | 2. Narrows Bridge |
3. Pedestrian Bridge | 4. Interchange Fountain |
5. Governor Kennedy Fountain | 6. Swan
Brewery | 7. St Georges College | 8. Matilda
Bay Tea Rooms | 9. Pelican Point Car Park |
10. Nedlands Baths Jetty

Start

Barrack Square.
This is the terminus for the
Blue CAT, and walking distance
from the city centre.

Finish

Corner Broadway and
The Avenue, Nedlands.
Buses 200, 201, 202 will take
you back to Perth city centre.

Length/Time

8 km/2.5–3.5 hours. The middle
section has very little shade,
so hot days should be avoided.

Wheelchairs

Not suitable for wheelchairs.

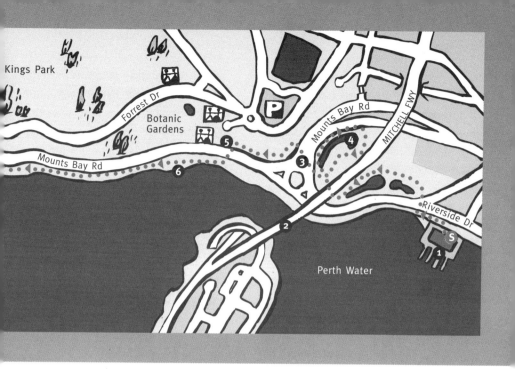

Walk No. 12

Mounts and Matilda Bays

Down the River—Barrack Street Jetty to Nedlands

This stretch of the river has always been important. Aboriginal people had major camping areas along the banks, and associated mythological stories. What is now Kings Park still dominates the modern city and river, with its more recent, European, history. The narrow strait (The Narrows) and the dominating Mt Eliza above it were important in determining the position of Perth. All of the original shallows next to the city have been reclaimed, especially for the freeway interchange next to the Narrows Bridge. Along the way the river bank changes from city to suburb, from highway verge to parkland. There are secluded nooks, historic sites, yacht clubs, the main university, birdlife, and—ever present—the river.

Go through the centre of **Barrack Square |1|** (see Walk 8 for details on the development of this area) towards the river, and then turn right, past piers providing services to Rottnest and along the Swan River. The Transperth jetty has frequent daily ferries to South Perth and the Zoo (see Walk 11). The entire Square is being redeveloped, and there are plans to build pools and a kiosk on the adjacent stretch of waterfront, facing Kings Park. Continue along the multi-purpose track by the edge of the river, towards the park. There is a sign for the Four Seasons Trail (with information stations that change during the year) which can be found within the bounds of the Narrows Interchange.

The interchange is where the Kwinana and Mitchell freeways meet to feed into the city, and can be seen straight ahead. Off to the right is the great wall of city highrises just beyond the Esplanade parkland with its pyramid conservatory (see Walk 2).

This whole riverfront area has been reclaimed from the river, which was mostly shallow and reed-fringed along its original shoreline. The overpass that appears from the right is where the William Street jetty used to be, poking out into deeper water. This was also the start of Mounts Bay, which has disappeared, totally filled in to accommodate the interchange.

The path goes along a built-up river wall, with good views ahead to Kings Park and Mt Eliza (see Walk 7), the red roofs of the old Brewery, the Narrows Bridge and across to the South Perth foreshore. The tall flag-pole, with Australian flag, was erected for the Australian bicentenary in 1988, but this walk turns right before that, through the tiled tunnel under part of the Freeway.

On the other side is a circular monument with several panels which illustrate the process of building the Narrows Bridge. Take the left hand path, signposted toward the **Narrows Bridge |2|**, past the first lake and a set of exercise equipment. Go through another tunnel, then past another lake. The south-bound traffic on the right is making its final approach to the bridge. Go left at the fork, avoiding the actual crossing, and then pass under the first span of the bridge, before curving back to the right along the other side of the freeway. A second bridge is being added, so there will be disruption, detours and construction vehicles here until the end of 2000.

Turn left, then immediately right before the **pedestrian bridge |3|**, to follow the path between the lake and the road on the left. This is Mounts Bay Road, approximately on the old shore line. The area below the Kings Park escarpment was used for market gardens in the early days, but these days it features hotels, apartments and a hospital/ medical complex.

The lake broadens just past the line of poplars to reveal a **fountain |4|** laid out in the shape of the stars of the Australian flag. It's a great sight with the city soaring up behind the columns of water. The jets and lights, when not in action, look like static ducks. There are lots of real birds here, including white-faced (grey) herons and cormorants. The track loops around this lake. Cross over the small bridge on the other side, to what seems to be an island. The path curves around, over a wooden bridge, and through a shady grove to a pair of small waterfalls. It is quite amazing, finding this tiny haven of nature tucked within Perth's major traffic complex.

The path eventually leads back to the pedestrian bridge where you now cross over Mounts Bay Road to the lower slopes of Kings Park. Looming straight ahead and above is Mt Eliza, with the Cenotaph peeping above. This is how the slopes of Gallipoli apparently looked, and why this is also known as Anzac Bluff (see Walk 7). On the other side of the bridge turn left then left again at the fork, to pass a lookout over the Narrows Bridge and a small limestone grotto. The path winds along the foot of the scarp for several hundred metres, with some of the rock face showing protective repair work, and separated from the road below by a bank of trees.

There are finally four steps leading down to a paved area surrounding the **Governor Kennedy Fountain |5|**. Immediately beyond the fountain is an open grassed area enclosed by some magnificent old plane trees, and beyond that the red brick pile of the old Swan Brewery.

This area was (and still is) of great significance to the local Aborigines, who called it Goonininup. This was a favoured meeting and camp site, with permanent springs and good seasonal feed. Traditional activities included fishing and crabbing in the river,

Opening Times

Matilda Bay Tea Rooms: daily 8am–8pm summer; 8am–5pm winter.

Refreshments

Café and restaurant near the start, the middle and end of the walk, and a hotel at the finish.

and honey gathering and wallaby hunting around Mt Eliza. There was also considerable mythological importance, being on the track followed by the Waugyl, the creator serpent. The principal story seems to be that the Waugyl lived on high ground near the current Parliament House, and travelled underground to emerge where Governor Kennedy's Fountain is, before crawling to the sea, creating the Swan River on the way.

The combination of fresh water and some level ground also encouraged European use of the site. In quick succession the open area was used for a boatyard, a feeding depot and then the Native Institute for the Aborigines (until they moved, or were driven, away from here), flour mill, Ticket of Leave Hiring Depot, and Old Men's Depot. In 1861 Governor Kennedy installed a cistern and pipe into the natural fountain, and 'a suitable drinking vessel' was provided by the Total Abstinence Association. Almost as a counter to this, the lower site was bought by the Swan Brewery in 1888, and a series of buildings erected over the next few years.

Go to the front of the fountain, and then citywards for a few metres, to where it's possible to cross the road. Do so, taking care to avoid the fast moving traffic. Turn right on to the mixed use path between the road and the river which then curls around the river side of the **Swan Brewery |6|**. This was not Perth's first brewery by any means (there were two established in the city by 1840), but the size of it reflected the grow-ing population and importance of Perth by the turn of the century.

The last twenty years have seen consid-erable controversy over the future of the site and the buildings. Many people saw the old brewery as an eyesore on the edge of Kings Park, and most Aboriginal people wanted it demolished to free up a site of considerable importance to them. Eventu-ally it was decided to retain it as a signifi-cant example of industrial architecture, and to refurbish it for modern commercial and tourist orientated retail use. There have been major delays, and concerns for traffic safety along the very busy Mounts Bay Road. However, it will probably re-open in 2000, though there is still uncertainty as to what it will be used for.

Carry on along the path next to the river, with extensive views across Melville Water, and back towards the Narrows Bridge and the city. The second small car park, on a tiny headland, signifies the entry to Matilda Bay, across which can be seen the

Lake and fountain in the heart of the freeway interchange.

masts of the Royal Perth Yacht Club, home for a few short years of the America's Cup, won by the yacht *Australia II* in 1983. Further to the right are the red tiled roofs and campanile of the University of Western Australia (UWA).

Further on and Kings Park gives way to the up-market suburb of Crawley, with its river view houses and tall apartment blocks (and solitary boathouse). These in turn give way, at Crawley Avenue, to the offices and residential halls of UWA.

On the left a sign announces the start of the Matilda Bay Reserve, and then the path turns left by Hackett Drive traffic lights. Off to the right can be seen the attractive

Gothic/Tudor brick pile of **St George's College |7|**. At the end of the car park, trees and lawn slope down to a narrow sandy beach. Matilda Bay has been a favourite picnic and bathing spot for over one hundred years. During summer, there's often a recreational boating hire service operating here, so people can paddle or pedal around the bay. Cut down towards the water, and walk along the edge of the grassed area, with the main UWA buildings off to the right (see Walk 13). Some stone terracing appears in front of the **Matilda Bay Tea Rooms |8|**, a good spot for some refreshment looking over boats and bay to the city.

Continue past two little-used wooden jetties with their access steps in the water (to keep cyclists off?). Keep to the water's edge in front of the spectacularly sited Matilda Bay Restaurant. There are great views to the city over still reflective water and bobbing yacht masts.

Continue as far as the boat ramp, then turn right through the car park. The grounds of the Royal Perth Yacht Club are on the left, while the red-bricked building on the right houses the headquarters of CALM (Department of Conservation and Land Management). At the end of the car park cross over the feeder road (called Australia II Drive), then turn half right over the grass to the concrete multi-use path.

Continue along this track, which winds through lawns, trees and small wetlands to the **Pelican Point car park |9|** and windsurfing area. Sailboards can often be hired here. The prevailing summer wind here is the sea breeze, a srong south–westerly which gives sailors here constant and consistent air. Sometimes they almost fly. But then, flying is a tradition here. This was the landing site of the Qantas Catalina Indian Ocean Service to Sri Lanka, and a plaque just beyond, surrounded by native shrubs, commemorates the flying boat service. The crew who manned these flights belonged to the Order of the Double Sunrise, because the trips were thirty hours long, nonstop and without radio contact.

The walk continues along the river's edge, past signs that refer to prawning. A local pastime is to pull nets through the shallows on summer evenings to catch the river prawns, and often to cook and eat them there on the beach.

The wooden jetty, with Jo-Jo's Café and Restaurant next to it, was opened in 1909 as the **Nedlands Baths Jetty |10|**. The river, and swimming in it, were major attractions in those days, and the Subiaco tram service terminated here. The jetty is used these days by restaurant patrons and hopeful fishermen. Another park is beyond the jetty, used for rugby matches in the winter and for kite flying when the wind is up.

Turn right up the narrow road/car park from the jetty, and then up the small hill, passing Steve's Nedlands Park Hotel, a popular watering hole for the past ninety years. The walk finishes here, by the intersection of Broadway and The Avenue. A bus stop is 200 metres up Broadway, past some cafés and restaurants.

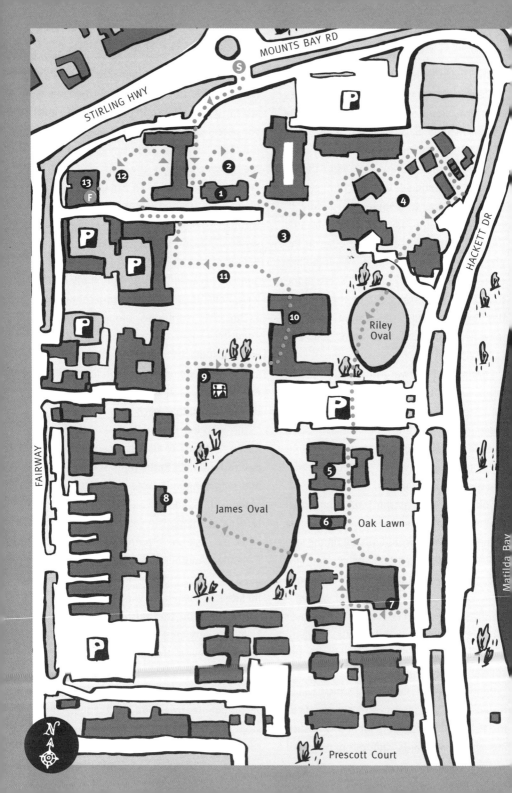

University of Western Australia

Campus delights: the groves of academe

Start

Main University entrance, corner Stirling Highway and Winthrop Avenue. Buses 70–73, 77, 78, from City Busport.

Finish

Lawrence Wilson Gallery. Buses 70–73, 77, 78 in Stirling Highway back to the city.

Length

3 km/about 2 hours

Wheelchairs

Diversions necessary at key Nos. |2|, |10| and |12|.

Walk key

1. Winthrop Hall | 2. Whitfield Court | 3. Moreton Bay Fig | 4. Somerville Auditorium | 5. Japanese Courtyard | 6. Berndt Museum of Anthropology | 7. Shenton House | 8. Irwin Street Building | 9. Reid Library | 10. New Fortune Theatre | 11. Tropical Grove | 12. Sunken Garden | 13. Lawrence Wilson Art Gallery

Perth's senior tertiary institution has one of the loveliest settings of any university campus. Set back from a large quiet bay of the Swan River, the university shows remarkable architectural consistency within glorious green surroundings. UWA promotes itself as a 'university without gates', and it provides a wonderful environment to walk or cycle through—and to be entertained or enlightened. There are six superb performance spaces, University Extension provides seasonal schools to bring courses and activities to the general community, and the Festival of Perth has its origins and home here. The gardens are recognised in the Register of the National Estate. It's really a series of gardens and groves within a greater garden, incorporating a variety of themes.

The start provides the first view of the spectacular **Winthrop Hall |1|** through a line of pencil-shaped cypresses. The entire vista, with the clock tower, the cloistered buildings on either side, and the open court, is superb.

Winthrop Hall is the heart and soul of the university, aesthetically and architecturally, and it dominates the campus from inside and out. It's the major feature of the Hackett Memorial Buildings, which include the structures to either side. The university owes much to Sir John Winthrop Hackett, co-owner and editor of the *West Australian* 1887–1916. He was a member of the Western Australia parliament and became the infant university's first Chancellor in 1912, when it opened in temporary buildings in Perth. His will left a large amount for the establishment of the campus here at Crawley. It was well spent.

Follow the driveway to the right, then turn left to pass in front of the Administration Building, half hidden behind its beautifully proportioned cloister (covered passage). The walls of the building feature a series of plaques with the emblems of the various arts and sciences. Directly in front is the creamy-gold Great Gate, with its leadlight windows and the colourful mosaic of the five 'lamps of learning' (Counsel, Courage, Wisdom, Understanding and Knowledge).

The entrance to Winthrop Hall is within the Great Gate, and the interior is worth looking at, providing that it's not in use. Pass through the foyer with its marble mosaic floor and beautiful vaulted brick ceiling. The hall's panelled walls have coats of arms from prominent universities around the world, and the great organ contains some 2,712 pipes, but the most appealing aspect is the ceiling. The massive beams are decorated with Aboriginal motifs, and some portraits which are only visible from the platform.

Come back out of the hall, turn right back through the gate, and down the adjacent steps to the middle of the large grassed area called **Whitfield Court |2|**, for another look at the hall. Note the three levels of Romanesque arches, the soaring clock tower, just like an Italian campanile, the coloured frieze, and the Reflection Pool. The busts and the stone benches either side of the pond, and their inscriptions, add to the overall effect. The Hackett Memorial Buildings were built between 1927 and 1931 with a Mediterranean theme. Most later developments on the campus followed this theme, with a uniformity of colour and texture through the use of terracotta tiles, limestone and concrete blocks. The overall balance is superb.

Continue across the court to a matching cloistered building, which houses a caféteria. A rose garden is to the left. Turn right through a large plain arch, and then left in front of a gigantic **Moreton Bay Fig |3|** which covers an area of over 1,500 square metres. There are over two hundred species of trees both indigenous and exotic, home to a wide range of birds whose calls echo around the campus.

The building straight in front is the Octagon Theatre, built in 1967, with input from Sir Tyrone Guthrie. It has a thrust stage, with seating on three sides for 650 people. It may be possible to look inside, but check at the box office or adjacent administration office.

You have now entered a small tree lined courtyard, known as Jackson Court. Behind a statue, '*The Dancer*', is a quiet grove of weeping peppermints, with a couple of jarrah trees. Follow the path between the Dolphin Theatre (small and intimate, with two hundred seats) and the Sports Centre, and then turn right into the **Somerville Auditorium |4|**. Note the massive wooden gateposts, and the gumnut insignia. This is one of the most wonderful places on the campus. It is laid out with tall Norfolk pines following the ground plan of a Gothic cathedral with nave and transept. As the exception that proves the rule there is a solitary soaring lemon-scented gum. This is one of the great spots on a summer evening, when the Festival of Perth runs its film season here, using rows of deckchairs.

Come out of the same gate and turn right to the Music Department. The first section houses the Eileen Joyce Studio, with its repository of early keyboard instruments. An attractive element of the studio is the glass wall facing on to the gardens of the Somerville Auditorium, and near the doorway a 'Composition of Earthenware Forms'. Continue and take the main corridor to the right through the department. Halfway along is a paved recess with a bust of the

Opening Times

Winthrop Hall: Mon to Fri 9am–5pm.
Music Department recitals: every Thurs at 1pm during the academic year.
Eileen Joyce Studio: First Mon every month (except January) 10am–1pm.
Berndt Museum of Anthropology: Mon, Wednesday 2pm– 4.30pm, Fri 10am–2pm.
Geology Museum: Mon, Wed, Fri 11am–6pm; Sun 12noon–5pm.
Lawrence Wilson Art Gallery: Tues to Fri 11am–6pm; Sun 12noon–5pm. Talks related to current exhibition, Tues 1pm.

Refreshments

Three cafeterias along the route.

composer and musician Percy Grainger, next to three North American swamp cypress.

Cut right through the small car park, between the brush walls of the Auditorium and University House (the staff club), to the edge of Riley Oval, the university's rugby ground. Nearby Matilda Bay (see Walk 12) can be seen off to the left. Cross the oval diagonally to the far corner of the Arts Building. Follow the crosswalk through the flame-tree framed car park, then half left into the covered walkway signposted to the Guild.

A short walk leads to the peaceful **Japanese Courtyard |5|**. A carp-filled pond is backed by limestone lumps, grassy knolls and Japanese style shrubs. These are actually indigenous plants, such as the Rottnest Island tea-tree, carefully pruned to Japanese shapes and sizes.

Next on the left is a large open area, called the Oak Lawn. This seems at first glance to be a misnomer, because, 'where are the oaks?' There are 450 species of oak (all bearing acorns) worldwide, and the lawn features the English, Algerian, pin and cork varieties. A small sign on the right points to the **Berndt Museum of Anthropology |6|**, which houses one of Australia's finest small collections of Aboriginal cultural materials.

Turn left down the far side of the Oak Lawn, and right around the end of the building (and past a cork oak). This is part of the Guild with refectory and bar. The next building is totally out of character. **Shenton House |7|** is one of Perth's oldest houses built about 1846, with additions in the 1850s and 1890s, and the cork oaks originally lined its driveway. Shenton, who was one of Perth's richest and most influential citizens, bought the property in 1878, and the government resumed the land on his death. It now features ugly heavy tiles and rotting gutters, and by an interesting quirk of fate houses the Centre for Aboriginal Programmes. Its principal decorative feature is the tiled floor in the main passage.

Go up the driveway past Shenton House, and into the South Entrance of Guild Village. Pass through the often student-

Winthrop Hall and its clock tower.

littered courtyard and then left towards the large open cricket ground, Riley Oval. Cross over to the attractive, low cream building on the other side of the oval.

This was the first home of the University, the **Irwin Street Building |8|** of 1913, reconstructed here to house the Cricket Club and the Archives department. Immediately to the right rear of the building is a small group of Western Australia Christmas Trees, so called because they produce a mass of golden blossom in December. This amazing tree is actually a parasite related to the ordinary mistletoe.

Follow the paved pathway through a large stand of marri trees, between the next group of buildings, past *'Seek Wisdom'*, up the steps and then right along the ramp to the **Reid Library |9|**. The design won a Bronze Medal in 1963 with its modern adaptation of the campus style. Toilets and caféteria are at ground level.

The full height balcony offers a good view of the Great Court. This tree lined courtyard links the library with Winthrop Hall and is part of the major north–south axis of the whole campus.

Continue along the walkway over to the next building, past another magnificent lemon-scented gum. Look through the branches to a small tower with a stylised swan windvane. Once in the Arts Building, go past 'Know Thyself', and left along the first passage. Continue past an open courtyard on the right, to the enclosed courtyard which is the **New Fortune Theatre |10|**, based upon the design of Shakespeare's Fortune Theatre. An unusual feature is a group of peacocks, who have made this their home, and occasionally enliven stage productions.

Just beyond the theatre go down the stairs, turning right at the bottom and out of the building. The Octagon Theatre can be seen to the right, but the walk goes half left to a giant 400 year-old jarrah tree. This area is the Great Court. Beyond the jarrah is a shady open grove of tall trees, the **Tropical Grove |11|**, flanked by two palms just behind a massive soaring New Zealand kauri.

Circle around the left hand side of the Tropical Grove until the Great Gate is in front of you. On the left is the cloistered Geography and Geology Building, and a chunk of local granite, 2,700 million years old. It puts us into perspective. Turn left around the Geology Department and go

past the Canary date palm to where there's a doorway under a small square tower. This is the entrance to the Geology Museum. The Eocene Garden is here, and it contains plants that have been largely unchanged for the last forty million years.

Cross back over the roadway to a dirt path leading through shrubbery to the open courtyard behind the Administration Building, with more plaques of the arts and sciences. You pass some strange neanderthal plants, which because of their charred black stems were formerly known as blackboys, but now are called grass-trees (*Xanthorrhoea*).

Circle through the courtyard and, at the far end, descend into a quiet, leafy enclosure. The **Sunken Garden |12|** is an Arcadian grove used occasionally for open air performances, and was the excavation site providing sand for the Hackett Memorial Buildings. A full sized Rottnest Island tea-tree can be seen next to the lily pond, while a poinciana (flamboyant) shades the sundial behind. This is part of the Shann Memorial, and the inscription around the curved stone seats came from a story Shann (a foundation professor) was told about a Maori leader.

Go between the seats and up the winding brick path to the **Lawrence Wilson Art Gallery |13|**, built in 1990 to house and exhibit the University's 2,500 artworks— which are well worth looking at.

This is the end of the walk. Behind the gallery an underpass leads to the highway where buses to Perth can be caught.

Subiaco

Subi: revitalised, trendy yet individual

Start

Corner Hay Street and Rokeby Road. Fremantle train to Subiaco, or buses 8, 9, 10, 11, 12, 13 (all travelling west along Wellington Street).

Finish

Subiaco Council Chambers, Rokeby Road. Buses 8, 10, 12 from Rokeby Road; 208, 209 from Hamersley Road back to Perth.

Length/time

5 km/2.5–3 hours

Wheelchairs

Detour around the Subiaco Theatre Centre.

Walk key

1. Regal Theatre | 2. Subiaco Station | 3. Subiaco Oval | 4. Victoria Hotel | 5. Park Street | 6. Stratmore | 7. Clock Tower | 8. Subiaco Theatre Centre | 9. Western Australia Medical Museum | 10. Timewells Store | 11. Subiaco Museum

Subiaco is a village within the city, with its own character, charm and ambience. Originally a working class suburb, Subiaco became trendy in the 1970s, but a strong sense of community and identity overcame threatened amalgamation and redevelopment. It retained its original single-storey houses, particularly the Federation house with its iron roof, bull-nose verandah, and leadlight windows.

Subiaco is the hospital suburb with three of Perth's major teaching hospitals, and it's the home of football, with Subiaco Oval being the venue for most of Western Australia's important Australian Rules games. An obsolete industrial area is being redeveloped as 'Subi Centro', with new housing, shops and parkland, all designed to complement the traditional character of Subiaco. Please note, the houses and gardens mentioned in this walk are private property, and should not be entered without permission.

Subiaco's main traffic intersection has always been at Hay Street and Rokeby Road. The tram from Perth once came along Hay Street and turned into Rokeby Road, around the Subiaco Hotel. The hotel, built in the 1890s, has been renovated, but unfortunately without the elegant spire damaged in the 1968 Meckering earthquake, and the verandahs don't have the same appeal as the original balconies.

Diagonally opposite the hotel is the art deco **Regal Theatre |1|**. In 1935 it replaced the open air Coliseum Picture Gardens, and was in danger itself of being pulled down until its owner (Paddy Baker, a real picture show man) created a trust to ensure its continuance. A fly tower has been built at the rear to accommodate most modern theatrical requirements.

The theatre is Perth's busiest, and possibly the busiest commercial (unsubsidised) theatre in Australia. The interior, unlike that of the Subiaco Hotel, has fortunately been left quite untouched and shows much of the art deco style.

In one corner of the foyer there's an old box office, still with tickets for one shilling and other pre-decimal prices. Pictures of the old movie stars, and posters of innumerable shows that have run at the Regal, adorn the walls. The 'Crying Room' is still there. Mothers used to park their babies in numbered stalls and, when one cried, the usher would call out 'Baby number seven crying', and the mother could go and comfort the child, while still watching the film through a window.

Proceed north along Rokeby Road away from the hotel. Near the end of the block on the right are the Rokeby Road and Subiaco Pavilion Markets. **Subiaco Station |2|** is just across Roberts Road and beyond it the Station Street Markets.

Subiaco is named after the town in Italy where the Benedictine Order was founded. The first Europeans in the area were Benedictine monks who settled around Lakes Monger and Herdsman, and called it New Subiaco. When in 1881 the railway from Fremantle to Perth was built, the station to the south of this settlement was called Subiaco. The suburb is often now referred to by its abbreviated name—Subi.

The entire area of the railway and beyond is being totally revamped in the Subi Centro plan. The railway line and station have been put underground, and the Station Square area is being transformed with shops, apartments and gardens. Most of the remaining area, stretching away to the left, will be medium density housing. Final completion of the entire project is scheduled for 2004.

Turn right into Roberts Road, past the rest of the Pavilion Markets. Across the road is a series of Moreton Bay figs which are being preserved. RR Imports, on the right, is on the site of the first house built (1886) in Subiaco. Because it was so far from town it was called 'Jones' Folly'. Its well later became important as a source of fresh water for the rapidly growing population brought in by the Gold Rush. Water was sold for a shilling a kerosene tin-full!

Turn first right, into Catherine Street, which has two sets of rare double-storey terraced houses built between 1904 and 1910 and recently restored. Note the decorative parapet on Nos. 18 to 32. The modern Kingdom Hall of the Jehovah's Witnesses, opposite, replaced a 1910 structure, but some of the original doors and windows were incorporated into the new building.

Continue to Hay Street, and turn left around the modern designer shopping centre, the Colonnade. Hay Street tends to have just a strip of shops with an occasional open arcade like Subiaco Mews across the road. Turn left into Axon Street and first right into York Street, which is now mixed residential and commercial. No. 232 is an untouched weatherboard house, while the small semi-detached cottages at Nos. 219 to 221 were typical workers' houses of the early 1900s. Turn left into Townshend Road and go to the next corner at Roberts Road, where 'Stranraer', a once grand, palm-fronted mansion, is sadly decaying.

Diagonally opposite from here is Western Australia's mecca of Aussie Rules football, **Subiaco Oval |3|**. The 65 metre light pylons are claimed to be the thinnest in Australia —every ground has to have its claim to fame. Cross Townshend Road (with the lights) to follow the grandstands along the other side of Roberts Road. Those who wish to look inside the ground should go to Gate 7 in Subiaco Road, the other side of the oval. Roberts Road has a series of

Opening Times

Subiaco Pavilion Markets: Thurs and Fri 10am–9pm; Sat and Sun 10am–5pm.
Subiaco Theatre Centre: 'Sundays at Subi' free concerts, summer only 3pm.
WA Medical Museum: Wed 10am–4pm, Sun 2pm–4pm.
Subiaco Museum: Thurs and Sun 2pm–4.30pm, Sat 10am–2.30pm.

Refreshments

Numerous cafés and restaurants along Rokeby Road and Hay Street, but few in the middle of the walk.

town houses and nondescript bungalows lurking behind high walls, to protect their inhabitants from traffic noise and the over-whelming presence of the oval.

Take the first street to the right, Ellen Street, and then left back into York Street. The first four houses on the left (Nos. 158 to 152) are very similar, each with two chimneys, but there are several variations in presentation. Go right into May Avenue, and right into Hay Street, around the Victoria Apartments a modern redevelop-ment of the area around the **Victoria Hotel** |4|. 'The Vic' itself was renovated, and a fairly plain 90 year old pub developed a new image, while retaining (and featuring) the original shape, roof and iron girders. It's now The Fish House, known as one of Perth's top eating places.

Cross over Hay Street (one way traffic from the left), and look back at 'The Vic'. Note the simple balcony, and the arched central chimneys. Proceed along Hay Street with the traffic flow and turn left into Olive Street, crossing Churchill, Barker and Park. There is a wide variety of housing styles, with Nos. 40 and 42, and 39 (and the modern replacement at No. 41), all one room width cottages on narrow blocks. Continue as far as No. 94 (Olive Cottage) which is a weatherboard cottage with an unusual outer wall of corrugated iron. It was supposedly shifted down from Kalgo-orlie by bullock cart and reassembled here. When big companies took control of the goldfields, individual miners left and some took their houses with them. It was the

The WA Medical Museum.

start of the Kalgoorlie Gold Rush of the mid 1890s that caused a significant growth in population and housing within Subiaco. Real estate speculation resulted in widely differing lot sizes and block widths, and several nonconnecting narrow streets.

Go back along Olive Street and turn left up **Park Street** |5|, specially paved in recog-nition of its unique character. Both sides of the road have stylish, picturesque cottages and houses (dating from the 1890s), full of colour, character and warmth. Note the variations in roofs, gables, fences, gates and verandah decorations.

Go left into Townshend Road and then right at the roundabout into Bagot Road.

No. 133, on the left, has remarkable Gothic and other decorative features, and is classified by the National Trust. Nos. 138, 140 and 155 are also worthy of note, all being preserved in original condition. The timberwork, used rather than iron lace, around the verandahs of Nos. 140 and 155 was due to the high cost of transport to then remote Subiaco.

Turn left into Robinson Street (continuation of Axon Street). This part of the suburb has been called the Subiaco Triangle — partly a real estate beat-up to increase desirability. Certainly these are tree lined streets with attractive houses, many of them renovated, and one section has been declared a conservation area by the National Trust. Continue over Hamersley Road into Chester Street, where No. 18, **'Stratmore' |6|**, could be considered as the grand old house of Subiaco. Built in 1905 it has superb pressed tin ceilings and is on the Register of the National Estate.

One of the appealing aspects of Subiaco houses is the use of leadlights, particularly in and around the front doors. This use of different coloured and textured pieces of glass (rather than stained glass) gives a magical feel, unfortunately only at night. The suburb claims to have Australia's largest concentration of leadlights, and has a Leadlight Festival every October.

Continue to Heytesbury Road, turning right and then right again into Salisbury Street. Go left into Hamersley Road, down to Rokeby Road. Diagonally opposite is the **Clock Tower |7|**, originally the Subiaco

Fallen Soldiers' Memorial, built in 1923 to commemorate those who fell in the Great War. The clock and bell still work, and the tower is the centrepiece of Subiaco's Anzac Day parade.

Behind the Tower are Rankin Gardens, named after an early Town Clerk, all set about with Norfolk pines, palms and rose beds. These are part of the central, largely green city square, an area that also takes in the Council Chambers and Library, the Subiaco Primary School, and the Subiaco Theatre and Theatre Gardens.

Continue along Hamersley Road. At No. 135 there is another stylish mansion, with an unusual small tower. The walk continues past the playing field of the Primary School to the **Subiaco Theatre Centre |8|**. This was originally the Civic Centre, a typically plain 1950s hall. Its relevance and usefulness diminished until in 1984 it was imaginatively converted to an intimate 300 seat theatre. Go into the ground floor foyer (toilets here) and up the stairs to what is now the main foyer and box office — or around the building if it's closed. Unfortunately staffing levels don't allow for viewing of the auditorium.

Go out the 'back' door, down the ramp to the gardens below. At the end of the ramp continue straight ahead to the next paved path. Go left past the ponds, then straight ahead across the lawns to the nearby street, Hensman Road. These are the Theatre Gardens, which during the Gold Rush were the site of a canvas 'Tiger' city, with the tents mostly made from Tiger Brand flour bags.

Turn right into Hensman Road and then left into Bagot Road, opposite the King Edward Memorial Hospital for Women, opened in 1939, with its splendid, green tiled art deco entrance. Come back along Bagot and continue down Hensman, then left at Barker Road to the **Western Australia Medical Museum |9|**. This was the original home of the Hospital. Domed turrets surmount the impressive entrance of this attractive limestone building, opened as an Industrial School for Girls in 1896. Designed by the great colonial architect George Temple Poole, it was converted to hospital use in 1916.

Go back up Barker Road past a series of flats and units which show how Subiaco might have developed if public action had not forced the preservation of the original character. Turn right up Raphael Street. Nos. 6 to 10 show interesting French roof influences (and baby Napoleons) in a modern terrace development. Across the road at No. 5 is a Tuscan style gateway to what was a double-storey bakery, since converted to a distinctive residence.

Return to Barker Road and continue in the same direction as before along to Rokeby Road. There is a wide variety of housing styles and ages. Note No. 366, with its limestone walls and doll's house gabled windows, and the half sunken house on the corner of Denis Street, a contemporary design featuring extensive use of recycled materials.

Cross over Rokeby Road to the Angus & Robertson corner, and turn around.

Directly opposite is Tighe's Building with an imposing parapet, built in 1905 as a grocery store. Stretching down Rokeby Road to the right is an attractive suburban shopping streetscape, much of it original.

Go up Rokeby Road to **Timewells Store** |10|, built in 1902 as King's Hall, a popular dancing spot. Timewells was recently renovated and the pressed tin ceilings, in original colours, of both hall and stage can be seen again. Continue up Rokeby Road, to where a small pedestrian mall has been transformed with a unique piece of public pavement art. The ceramic snake celebrates Subiaco's centenary and symbolises both the Aboriginal and European contributions to the area. The tail of the snake contains 140 tiles made by local school children, with images from the history and life of Subiaco.

Further up Rokeby Road is the major intersection with Bagot Road. One corner houses the relatively modern Crossways Shopping Centre, and opposite is Doyle Court from 1904. Another corner has a service station, and the fourth has the Subiaco Library, where the original post office and fire station once stood.

Cross over to the library corner and proceed along Bagot Road to the Subiaco Primary School. This was another George Poole design from 1897, and the school has recently been given a new lease of life with major extensions. The tall gums in front of the school are a favourite resting spot for black cockatoos whose squawking often fills the evening air.

Return to Rokeby Road turning right past the Library. A stone set here in the lawn commemorates the site of the original Council Chambers and Literary Institute. The new, functional Council offices are along the brick paved path leading to the left, but straight in front, across the lawn, is the **Subiaco Museum |11|**. Housed in an old electricity substation, it contains early maps and photographs of Subiaco and other memorabilia, including the entire facade (with verandah) from an old Park Street weatherboard house.

This is the end of the walk. There is a bus stop on the street here, and the railway station is at the foot of Rokeby Road.

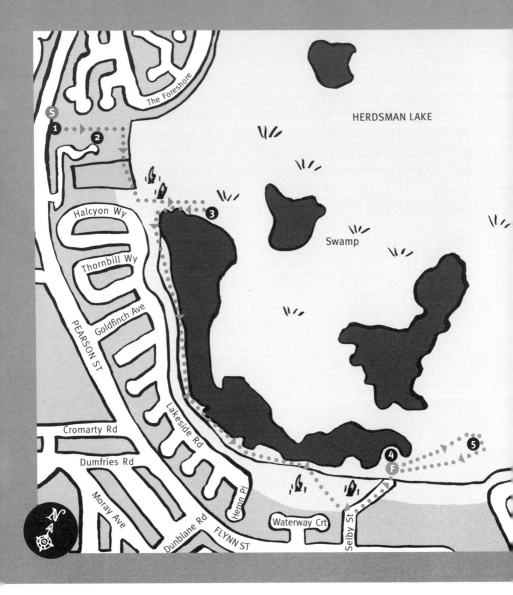

HERDSMAN LAKE

The Foreshore

Halcyon Wy

Thornbill Wy

Goldfinch Ave

PEARSON ST

Cromarty Rd

Dumfries Rd

Moray Ave

Lakeside Rd

Heron Pl

Dunblane Rd

FLYNN ST

Waterway Crt

Selby St

Swamp

Walk key

1. Settler's Cottage | **2.** Herdsman Main Drain | **3.** Nature Trail |
4. Herdsman Lake Wildlife Centre | **5.** Gould League Walk

Walk No. 15

Herdsman Lake

A stroll along the edge of one of Perth's wetlands

Start

Herdsman Lake Settler's Cottage, Pearson Street, Churchlands. Catch either bus 92 (travelling west along Wellington Street) or 401 (from the City Busport) to Pearson St (the stop before Hale Road).

Finish

Herdsman Lake Wildlife Centre. Take buses 92, 401 from corner Flynn/Selby streets back to the city.

Length/Time

4 km/1.5–2 hours. Early morning and late afternoon are best for optimum wildlife sighting, and to avoid midday sun as there is limited shade on the walk.

Wheelchairs

Access is generally good, but you will encounter some rough surfaces.

Herdsman was the biggest of the 'Great Lakes' that originally lay just to the north of newly settled Perth. Most of these, and many others along the coastal plain, have since been drained. The remaining wetlands are very important for retaining biodiversity, and are significant bird sanctuaries. About eighty-five species, including migratory waders from Siberia, are normally seen at Herdsman. There's also a variety of frogs, spiders, insects and reptiles. The Gould League of Western Australia maintains a Wildlife Centre on the edge of the lake.

The walk follows the edge of the lake along to the Wildlife Centre. Much of the lake area is covered by bulrushes but there is a significant amount of permanent open water.

Settler's Cottage |1| is the only remainder of a local settlement scheme. Such schemes were common in the 1920s and 1930s, and this was a government designed 'Type Three Cottage', timber-built with an asbestos roof. It's small and basic, but adequate, and has been furnished in simple 1930s style. Look in through the windows if the cottage is shut. The settlement scheme probably followed the building of the Herdsman Lake Tunnel between 1921 and 1925. This was to partially drain the lake, to enable ex-servicemen to develop market gardens on the newly exposed fertile alluvial soil.

A path leads down the back of the property from the rear of the cottage, between an open ditch to the right and an enormous pile of sand to the left. The sand is in anticipation of a major road which may be constructed through here some time well into the future. The ditch is the first part of what is officially known as the **Herdsman Main Drain |2|**, with the tunnel portion only starting over the other side of Pearson Street. The drain/tunnel was built to lower the level of the lake (which has no natural exit) by draining some of the water away to the sea, through the intervening ridges and dunes. No pumping is required as the drain is 6 metres above sea level here.

Go through an unlocked gate at the bottom of the garden (close it behind you), and turn right to cross the small bridge over the drain. From the bridge, continue straight on along the pathway. Bear left at the next fork to stay close to the reed covered (and

The bird haven at Herdsman Lake.

hidden) lake shore. The path curves around some trees to approach open water, next to which is a **Nature Trail |3|** sign.

Follow this trail, along a line of trees, mostly paperbarks, and on to the boardwalk. Do not proceed beyond the end of the boardwalk, unless the trail has obviously been upgraded and the bulrushes cut back. This is a favourite haunt of tiger snakes. Heed the numerous warning signs. The trail marks the start of a broad stretch of open water, on which a range of birds can usually be seen, with the city towers over in the distance.

Come back to the main path and continue along it. A series of exclusive suburbs starts on the right, taking the place of the market gardens that have been progressively pushed further and further out of town. The entire lake shore has, however, been kept as a public reserve.

The path meanders for quite some distance across rolling lawns that lead down to reeds, occasional stands of paperbarks, and the water. There are a few small shaded lookouts, a couple of children's playgrounds, and benches for just sitting and looking, and maybe dreaming. Some of these are strategically placed beneath casuarinas (she-oaks) where the breeze soughs as it murmurs through the needles.

Ducks and swans, pelicans, ibises, gulls, cormorants, swamphens and coots, herons, honeyeaters, wagtails, ravens, magpie larks and harriers—and even the odd goose—can all be seen doing whatever it is that birds do. It's a delightful stretch for a gentle stroll.

The path curves away where a small drainage canal leads into the lake. Cross over the small footbridge and left along the driveway to the **Herdsman Lake Wildlife Centre |4|**, keeping to the left of World Wide Fund for Nature (WWF) Panda Cottage. The centre has a number of displays and information sheets about the lake and its wildlife, including recognition charts to help identify the birds and plants. There's also a viewing area up the stairs, 5 metres above the lake level, for observing the passing parade.

Come back out of the main entrance and turn left across the lawn, between the centre and the WWF's offices on the right,

Opening Times
Herdsman Lake Settler's Cottage:
Sat, Sun and public holidays 2pm–4pm. (Small entry fee.)
Herdsman Lake Wildlife Centre:
Mon–Fri 8.15am–4.30pm; Sat and Sun 1pm–4.30pm. (Small entry fee.) There's a conducted bird walk on the third Sat of every month, at 7am. For details, phone 9387 6079.

Refreshments
Only at the Wildlife Centre (when open) and nearby shops at end of walk. Toilets the same.

to a built up pathway. If the centre is closed, circle the building in a clockwise direction, then veer left to the path.

This is the **Gould League Walk |5|** and takes a looping trail, part gravelled path and part boardwalk, through paperbarks and reeds, to quiet lookouts over the lake. It's full of birds and flitting dragonflies, melodious birdsong, mysterious splashes and rustling bulrushes, with cool shade, glimpses of houses, and distant, muted traffic noise. This part should not be rushed.

The trail leads back to the Wildlife Centre where the walk ends. Buses and shops can be found in Flynn Street at the top of the Wildlife Centre driveway.

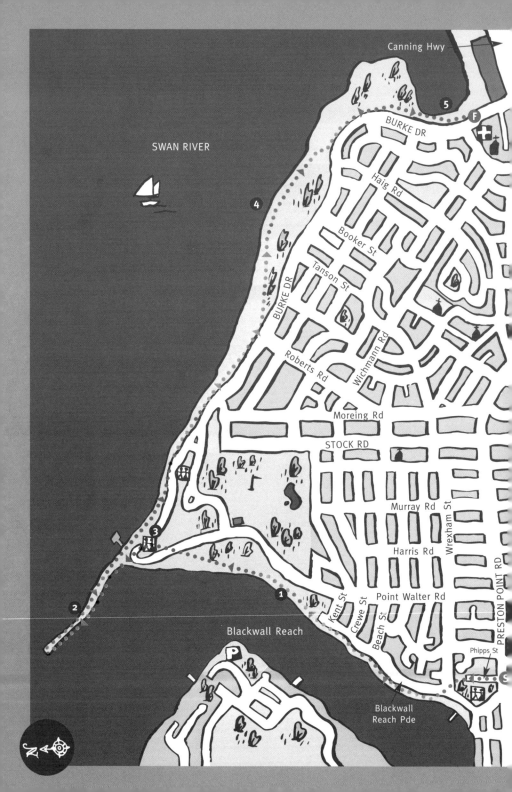

Point Walter

A riverside stroll along limestone cliffs and sandy shallows

Start

Corner Preston Point Road and Phipps Street, Bicton. Buses 148 or 158 ex Fremantle Railway Station; or 158 ex-Perth City Busport.

Finish

Corner Burke Drive and Lentona Road, Alfred Cove. Buses 106, 158 run between Perth and Fremantle.

Length/Time

6.5 km (plus 1–1.5 km for Point Walter spit)/2 (2.5) hours. Late afternoon gives best views of city, and of twilight sailing between November and April.

Wheelchairs

Some steep slopes. Avoid grass and sand areas at Point Walter.

Walk key

1. Blackwall Reach | 2. Point Walter sand spit | 3. Paved Pedestrian Mall | 4. Swan Estuary Marine Park | 5. Alfred Cove

When early explorers made their way up the Swan River from Fremantle by boat they traversed a relatively narrow river, through some cliff-lined reaches, before rounding a long sandy spit and then entering a surprisingly broad open stretch of water. This was Melville Water, in effect a large lake several kilometres wide. At the far end the Swan passed through the aptly named Narrows, beneath Mt Eliza.

This walk goes along Blackwall Reach through natural bush, above limestone cliffs as far as the Point Walter spit. It then follows the shallow, open south bank of Melville Water, whose waters are alive with boats through the warmer months. Scudding sails make a picturesque foreground for the distant tall towers of Perth.

Walk down Phipps Street (past the adjacent park) as far as it goes, and turn left into another small park towards the river below. Take the first fork left to a lookout with views over the baths and jetty and downstream towards Fremantle. The first settler in 1830, John Duffield, operated a lime kiln here, and named the property after Bicton in Devon.

Follow the path as it curves back to the right, to a heritage trail plaque (there are several along the way), where there's a clear view across the river to an enormous series of limestone walls. This was for many years the grand site of the old CSR sugar refinery, now about to be an even grander housing estate.

Zigzag down the path, ignoring a fork to the left, cross the road, and then turn right along the concrete path at the water's edge. Just offshore are numerous boats on permanent moorings well clear of the main river channel. There are several little beaches along this stretch, many with dinghies drawn up on the sand, while very stylish, view-filled houses line the road along the right hand side.

The path starts climbing alongside the start of Blackwall Reach Parade, and several seriously expensive mansions appear on top of a limestone crag high up to the right. All of these riverside suburbs are, as the estate agents put it, highly desirable.

Carry on down to the aptly named Beach Street. Across the river are the dark green glass boxes of the Chidley Point Golf Club. There is another small beach, and jetty, below Kent Street, a popular spot for families with young children during summer.

At the end of the houses and road, follow the fenced concrete path into the riverside bushland. This is where **Blackwall Reach |1|** really begins, with steep, rough pockmarked cliffs, where the Swan has cut through a limestone ridge. It was named by a Royal Navy commander after Blackwall Reach on the Thames, though the resemblance is hard to see.

Fourteen hectares of shoreline have been put into the Blackwall Reach Reserve, to maintain what is a relatively untouched part of the Swan Valley. Remnant bush, which still has some large tuart trees, covers the strip of land behind the cliffs, which represent the best preserved section of river limestone in Perth. The river traffic has a speed limit here of 8 knots.

Take the first gravel path down to a timber platform looking out over the river. There is a descriptive sign, and good views along the cliffs in both directions, and directly opposite is the small sandy beach of Chidley Point. Go down to each of the subsequent lookouts. Despite the warning signs these are favourite spots for high diving and jumping—the cliffs are up to 9 metres high. There is a track and steps up from the river by the third platform (signposted Clifftop Decks), to enable jumpers to do it again, and again.

Go back to the concrete path and continue in the same direction. The track winds through more bush, with parrot bush, peppermint trees, grass-trees, banksias, and interrupted views down to the broadening river. Eventually the path returns to the road, by an information shelter. Cross the road, and then go left across the lawns to the circular stone lookout. The **Point Walter sand spit |2|** can be clearly seen on the left, stretching far out into the Swan, while off to the right is the expanse of Melville Water.

Go straight down the slope, past the car park, to the broad patch of sand, which is Point Walter, and the start of the spit. A sign explains how at one time a channel was cut through here, to reduce the sailing time along the river. Go out along the spit, as far as the tide (or your confidence) will allow. Bear in mind that the tidal range here is only half a metre. Off to the left (of the spit) are some of Perth's most exclusive houses, rising up the steep slopes of Mosman Park. Moving round to the right there are the masts and clubhouse of the Royal Freshwater Bay Yacht Club, with well-treed and well-heeled Peppermint Grove beyond, high above the enclosed Freshwater Bay. There are several blocks of highrise apartments at the head of the bay, which leads round to another elite suburb, Dalkeith. The nearest bit of land, backed by yet another riverside park, is Point Resolution. At one time there was serious consideration given to building a bridge between Points Walter and Resolution. That would really have put the cat among the (wealthy) pigeons.

Come back along the spit and past the small jetty, a favourite fishing and bathing spot. The river, for the rest of the walk, has

Opening Times

Point Walter sand spit: Readily walkable only at low tide – see daily paper, *The West Australian*, for low tide times.

Point Walter Café: 9am–5pm daily throughout the year, closing later on summer weekends.

Refreshments

Point Walter café is the only outlet (and only toilet) along the walk. Others in Canning Highway close to the walk end.

a gently sloping bank, making it very safe for swimming. The brown jellyfish seen in the river have an extremely mild sting, felt only on sensitive skin.

Enter the **paved pedestrian mall |3|** which stretches across the front of some public barbecues, a playground, café and kiosk, showers and toilets, with rolling lawns all around. This is a favourite picnic area on summer evenings and fine weekends throughout the year. The exit (which is usually the entrance) of the paved mall, of the Point Walter Reserve, has a series of twelve mosaics depicting activities here over the years. This leads into a large car park. Cross over to the grass by the water's edge and turn right along the river, which here is the beginning of a designated water-skiing zone. A little further on there is a jet ski area. There are good views across the river to Perth's most expensive address—Jutland Parade in Dalkeith. This street at one time boasted Australia's highest priced house.

At the end of the long car park, cross over a short road leading to a boat ramp, and continue along the concrete pathway, separated from the river by a strip of trees and sedgegrass. The tall towers of Perth start to appear across the broad Melville Water. This stretch of the walk is a gentle stroll along 3 kilometres of parkland fringing the river. There are a few features worth highlighting, with most of the walk just there to be enjoyed.

A sign identifies the **Swan Estuary Marine Park |4|** which protects the inshore waters here, while the coastal strip is in the Alfred

A pelican in the shallows of Melville Water.

Cove Nature Reserve. The path curves away from the road, to a more secluded presence along the foreshore, then through a stand of pine-like casuarinas to a plaque on the site of the long gone Attadale Jetty. The park widens out to form a broad grassy area, and there are views to the next headland on this side of the river. This is Point Dundas, also known as the Majestic Hotel site. The Majestic was one of Perth's best known art deco hotels but was demolished some years ago, and is now the site of numerous expensive and ostentatious houses. Over on the other side of the river the first of a series of yacht clubs can be seen. The tall towers of the city beyond sit comfortably between the twin green wedges of Kings Park and South Perth.

Melville Water provides an ideal sailing location, with ample room for the boats of several clubs. The mixed sails and colours are a splendid sight on weekends, and on summer evenings when the largely social 'twilight sails' take place. The boats and distant buildings have an extra glow in the intense colours of late afternoon.

This area is a favourite haunt for cyclists and walkers, many with dogs, as the track wends its way past benches and small clumps of trees. Both bay and path curve right to another plaque, for the old Brick Landing Site. An area of shallows just out in the bay is a favourite pelican haunt. The path goes through an area of trees next to the road (by the Burke Drive/Haig Road intersection), then passes some playing fields (Troy Park). The river curves back in at this point, to create the quiet, sheltered, shallow backwater of **Alfred Cove |5|**. It's a haven for birds, despite the nearby Canning Highway, one of Perth's main traffic arteries.

The walk ends at the junction of Burke Drive and Lentona Road, by the last of the Melville Heritage Trail markers. Canning Highway, with buses back to Perth or Fremantle, is just a short distance up Lentona Road.

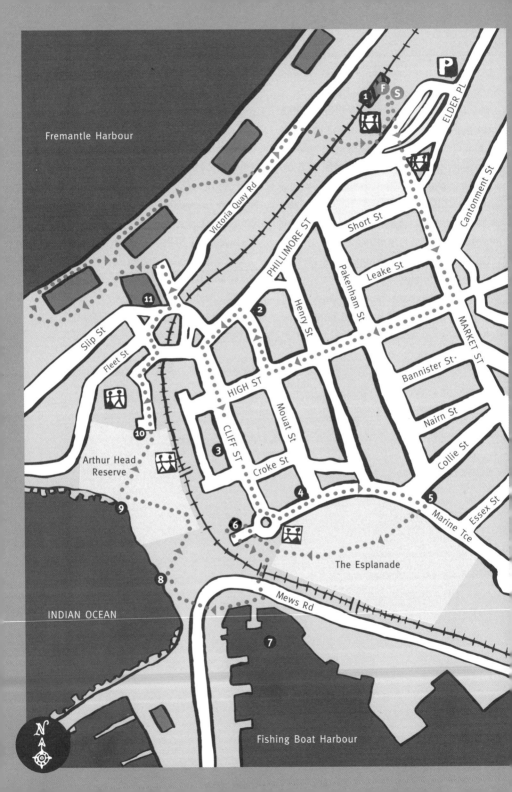

Fremantle Harbour

P

1 F S

ELDER PL

Cantonment St

Short St

PHILLIMORE ST

Leake St

Pakenham St

Henry St

MARKET ST

Victoria Quay Rd

11

2

HIGH ST

Bannister St

Slip St

Fleet St

CLIFF ST

Mouat St

Nairn St

Collie St

10

3

Croke St

4

5

Arthur Head
Reserve

9

6

Marine Tce

Essex St

8

The Esplanade

INDIAN OCEAN

Mews Rd

7

Fishing Boat Harbour

N

Fremantle–Port City

Stepping along the old streets and shorelines of Western Australia's major port

Start

Fremantle Railway Station. Take the train (Fremantle line), or buses 105, 151, 159, leaving from the City Busport.

Finish

At the starting point. The same trains and buses return to Perth.

Length/Time

3.5 km/2–2.5 hours

Wheelchairs

Several sets of steps make this walk unsuitable for wheelchairs.

Walk key

1. Fremantle Railway Station |
2. His Majesty's Hotel | 3. Lionel Samson & Son | 4. Old Court House | 5. Esplanade Hotel | 6. Maritime Museum | 7. Fishing Boat Harbour | 8. Long Jetty | 9. Bathers Bay | 10. Round House | 11. Fremantle Port Authority

Fremantle, at the mouth of the Swan River, is where the first British settlers landed. A major difficulty was a rock bar at the river mouth which prevented any access from the sea, until it was eventually blasted and the harbour created.

When convicts were introduced, Fremantle was where they landed and built many heritage landmarks. This is also where European migrants arrived —and stayed. Their influence still exists.

Time and developments passed Fremantle by, until 1987 when the defence of the America's Cup led to the entire city being refurbished. Fortunately the nature and scale of the place wasn't changed, leaving a rich repository of history and architecture.

Fremantle Railway Station |1| is an attractive and decorative building, built in 1906. Follow the pedestrian crossing, through the station forecourt and over Phillimore Street, to Market Street. Turn to look back at the station before proceeding up Market Street. The Spare Parts Puppet Theatre is behind the small park on the right, and the solid 1907 Post Office, with its bands of white plaster and red brick, straight ahead. A little further on, across the road, is the typically plain Wesley Church, built in 1888 and now part of the Uniting Church.

There are two interesting shops on either side of Leake Street. The Princess Hairdressing Salon has housed a salon and tobacconist since 1909, and many of the original fittings are still there. The side window still advertises 'Maritana Cigars 6d'. Kakulas Sister is opposite. Like its big brother in Northbridge (see Walk 5) it is full of exotic smells and produce.

Continue to the traffic lights at High Street, and turn right around the National Hotel, with its precise tuck pointed brickwork and plaster faces above the window arches. High Street has one of Western Australia's finest streetscapes, with a splendid collection of two and three storey buildings. They show a wide variety of ages and styles, many from the late 1890s and early 1900s, with imposing pediments and balustrades, classical arches and decorative plasterwork. It's worth zigzagging along the street in order to appreciate both sides, but note the one way traffic from behind you.

There's also a wide range of shops, with several galleries (including Aboriginal art) to distract you. Hotels feature strongly, reflecting the proximity to the port. The street has, however, lost much of its earlier rollicking sailor's style. No. 82, the Hospital Benefit Fund, was built as a bank, while balconies have been added on the original exterior of the Orient Hotel.

This family hotel has been beautifully redecorated and is worth a quick look inside. The Coakleys (ex Cleopatra) and P&O hotels (with its turbaned pillars) have their own character, while the Challenge Bank (No. 22) has a solid but stylish dependability. This was originally the Western Australian Bank, one of many Fremantle buildings designed by Talbot Hobbs, who was also responsible for the Cenotaph at Kings Park (see Walk 7).

Turn right here into Mouat Street. At No. 5 there is an unusual and highly individualistic limestone structure, which at different times housed the German Consulate and a night club. Across the road are old warehouses, now adapted to modern usage, and with their plaster work picked out in Federation colours.

Continue along Mouat Street, to **His Majesty's Hotel |2|**. There is a short line of sand coloured bricks, with outlines of fish, crabs, shells and starfish, within the pavement. It continues across the lawn to the left, and along the pavement just around the corner. This shows where the old shoreline ran, and appears on several places during the walk. This was originally the edge of

North Bay on the Swan River, while there was South Bay on the seaside. Both bays have since disappeared under reclaimed land.

Cross over to the other side of Phillimore Street and turn around to admire a marvellous set of buildings. In front is His Majesty's, the Howard Smith Building is to the right, half hidden by trees, then the impressive P&O Building, round to the domed Wilhelmsen (which was originally Elders, a major Australian pastoral trading company) House, another Hobbs design. Over to the left is the current, modern Customs House, cunningly concealed behind preserved 19th century facades.

Turn away from this Customs House, to pass around the previous 1909 version, the brick and stucco building on the corner. Cross over Phillimore Street to go left along Cliff Street, past Wilhelmsen House. The interior has a high arched foyer with a split staircase beneath a high glass dome.

Continue to High Street, and look left to the high tower of the Fremantle Town Hall, then right to Western Australia's oldest building, the Round House, which you will visit later in the walk. The boarded-up archway at the foot of the staircase is the exit to the tunnel which runs through from the beach beyond—and should be reopened in the near future.

Continue along Cliff Street, past a preserved facade (Fremantle has very strict heritage retention laws) on the right, and the Portuguese Consulate at No. 22, before reaching the offices of **Lionel Samson & Son |3|**. The Samson family has been a

Opening Times

Maritime Museum: (donation entry) daily 10.30am–5pm.
Round House: (donation) November to April 9am–6pm, May to October 9am–5pm.
Fremantle Port Authority: Observation Deck tours (free) Mon–Fri 1.30pm.

Refreshments

Several cafés and restaurants along the route.

significant force in Fremantle since settlement. Lionel came out to Western Australia in 1829, when he bought this land and established a liquor trading company, which is now the longest continuously owned family business in Australia. A grandson, Sir Frederick Samson, was Fremantle's Lord Mayor for twenty-one years, and had much to do with the careful preservation of its heritage. These ornate Gold Rush offices, with their wire pigeon deterrents, were built by Hobbs, while the plain stone structure next door was the Samson home, built in 1835.

The pavement of Croke Street shows the old shoreline of South Bay, demonstrating the short distance that existed between the two bays. On the right hand side of Cliff Street is an unpretentious stone and brick building. The central single storey section, was convict built in 1852 as the Government Commissariat.

Western Australia was originally a free colony, but development stalled and convicts were brought in to revitalise the struggling economy. The first convicts arrived here in Fremantle in 1850 and were immediately put to good use (see Walk 18). The Commissariat is now part of the Maritime Museum, which you will visit later.

Continue along Cliff Street, to where a small laneway exists at the rear of a group of semi-detached houses. Three 'dunnies', or outdoor toilets, can be seen there—they have been retained for their heritage value!

Continue left around to the front of these houses, in Marine Terrace. The porticoed

The Round House, Perth's oldest building.

entrances lead into what were the Water Police Barracks. The classical structure just beyond was the **Old Court House |4|**, constructed by convict labour in the 1880s. It's now part of Notre Dame University, which is the only Roman Catholic, and the only town (that is, not a dedicated campus) university in Australia. Some 1,200 students are taught in seventeen different renovated buildings in the few blocks just behind the Court House. It is a great new usage for an old area.

Carry on along Marine Terrace, past Mouat and Henry streets, and then following what was the old shoreline. It's a strange feeling to know this was once lapped by the sea, which now is out of sight. At the next intersection is Artisans of the Sea, a stylish outlet for Broome pearls. Across the road is the elegantly domed and balconied **Esplanade Hotel |5|**. Warehouses here were used as the first convict depot in 1850, and this late 19th century corner pub was renovated, and extended along to the next street, in the lead up to the America's Cup defence.

Cross over Marine Terrace opposite Collie Street, into the Esplanade Reserve, and head half right between the two lines of pines. There are two memorials, the first erected to three explorers killed by Aboriginals, with a later plaque commemorating the twenty Aboriginals killed by the subsequent punitive party. Further on is a curved metal and ceramic monument to Portuguese navigator, Vasco da Gama for opening up the Indian Ocean.

At the end of the park, cross back through the car park to the **Maritime Museum |6|**, which is housed in the old Commissariat/Government Stores complex. This group of buildings was later used by the Customs Department and the Post Office, before being refurbished for its museum usage. Entry is by donation, to view relics of shipwrecks around the Western Australia coast, especially the reconstruction of the *Batavia* and its cargo. The Museum is also an internationally recognised Centre for Excellence for its expertise in marine archaeology and preservation.

On leaving the Museum go straight ahead from the entrance to the pedestrian railway crossing. Go through and over the road into the restaurant area (this is a great place to stop for fish and chips), continuing through the car park to the wooden decking around the **Fishing Boat Harbour |7|**. Depending on the time and the season there may be dozens of fishing boats tied up at the wharves.

This is where the statue of Our Lady of the Sea is paraded every November, and taken out to sea for the Blessing of the Fleet by the Catholic Archbishop. This is, as much as anything, a celebration of the cultural background of Fremantle. Migrants from the Mediterranean countries of Greece, Italy and Portugal have had great influence on the character, trades and traditions of the city.

Fremantle's first jetty, the South Jetty, jutted out here into South Bay. Goods were landed here, then shifted along Cliff Street to North Bay, for shipment upriver to Perth.

Move left along the decking to Cicerello's Landing for a view through to the yacht masts in Success Harbour. The foreground is where many of the America's Cup contestants had their boatsheds during the races of 1987. The 'Auld Mug' had been won by *Australia II* in 1983 in the USA, and the defence was in the waters just offshore from here four years later, when the Americans won it back.

Turn back and go to the front of McDonald's. The timber structure on the beach, with its information plaques and maps, is a remnant of **Long Jetty |8|**. This replaced South Jetty, and eventually stretched one kilometre out to sea. Mostly demolished in 1921, a few pylons can still be seen out in the bay. Go around McDonald's, past a blue mosaic bollard marking the location of Angelsea Point, then following the old shoreline to a coloured map which shows the original shoreline and the subsequent developments of the Arthur Head Reserve.

Follow the old shoreline again towards the tall flagpole, and then fork left to stay below the headland. This is **Bathers Bay** |9|, where the first settlers from the *Parmelia* landed in 1829 and had to camp among the midwinter dunes while land was surveyed and allocated. The Round House was built above here just two years later as the first gaol. Priorities!

At the foot of the cliff is the boarded-up Whalers' Tunnel, which runs through to High Street. A whaling station operated here for a few years, and the tunnel enabled easy access to Fremantle. Funds have been allocated for repair work on Arthur Head and the Round House, which will allow the tunnel to be reopened.

Go back to the start of the headland, turning left up the steps and slope to the **Round House** |10|. This twelve sided limestone structure had just eight cells, used only for local convicts (none of that overseas riffraff!), some of them Aboriginals, many en route to Rottnest (see Walk 21). The building fell into disuse until restoration in 1974, by when some of the cells had gone for good.

Fremantle Heritage Guides are usually in attendance to provide information on the Round House and the Gun Deck outside. There used to be a time ball tower (as at

Greenwich), and there's still a 1pm ceremony where the gun is fired and the black ball dropped. The flagpole is in fact the spare mast from the yacht *Australia II*.

Arthur Head is the last remnant of a limestone ridge that stretched from Angelsea Point (left) to the original Arthur's Head, approximately where the black cranes are to the right. The rest of the ridge was removed for a battery of guns (Fort Arthur) and to create the new harbour, with the debris used for moles and reclamation.

Go to the front of the Round House. There is a clear view down the length of High Street from here and, in the foreground, two examples of heritage buildings converted to apartments. The tall glass frontages, immediately below on the right, define the doorways of the old Fremantle Municipal Tramways Car Barn.

Carry on down the other side of the Round House. The old cottages here were harbour master and pilot houses. The first now houses a café and a tourist information office. The last cottage was occupied by a pilot called Trivett. He and then his wife were allowed to stay on after retirement, and so the short road is called Mrs Trivett Place.

Turn right down here, then half left and round to the front of the tall modern structure of the **Fremantle Port Authority** |11|. This is the nerve centre for both the Inner Harbour within the river mouth and the Outer Harbour further south in Cockburn Sound. The foyer has historic photographs and other memorabilia, and a Wind and

Tide display. There are weekday tours of the Observation Deck ten storeys up. The statue in front is of C. Y. O'Connor, Western Australia's great engineer who was responsible for the Goldfields Water Scheme (see Walk 24) and the railway route through the Darling Range (see Walk 23).

He also designed Fremantle's Inner Harbour. When he arrived the plan was to build a harbour into the sea, like the Long Jetty, and with the same susceptibility to bad weather. O'Connor devised a scheme to blast the rock bar at the mouth of the Swan, and create two lines of wharves along the dredged river banks, with protective moles extending out to sea. The scheme worked, and the harbour today is pretty much as he created it. Across the road is the bow of the submarine HMAS *Oxley*. The slots were for the firing of torpedoes and missiles.

Turn left towards the harbour, cutting across to 'A' Shed with its bar and café, a good spot to rest. This whole area is due for redevelopment between 1999 and 2001 as part of a grand plan to create a Maritime Precinct. The space beyond 'A' Shed, where the original Arthur's Head was, is to have a new Maritime Museum providing a permanent home for exhibits of Western Australia's maritime history, including *Australia II*.

Come back to the gap between 'A' and 'B' sheds, displaying anchors from ships that have foundered near here. 'B' Shed houses the office of Sail Training Ship *Leeuwin*, whose mooring is alongside. The *Leeuwin* is a modern square rigger used for environmental and personal development voyages. Part of 'B' Shed may have some maritime heritage displays. Continue past the *Leeuwin* mooring to the Ferry Terminal, with connections to Rottnest (see Walks 21 and 22), and then go half right across the car park, towards the railway pedestrian bridge. On the other side turn left, past a blue bollard which marks an old river crossing point, back to the station where the walk ends.

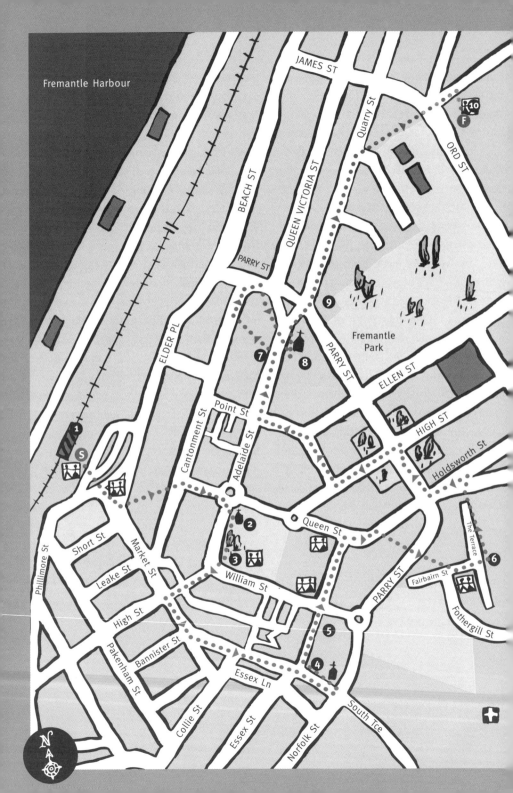

Fremantle Harbour

JAMES ST

Quarry St

ORD ST

F
10

BEACH ST

QUEEN VICTORIA ST

PARRY ST

9

ELDER PL

Fremantle Park

7

8

PARRY ST

ELLEN ST

Cantonment St

Point St

Adelaide St

HIGH ST

Holdsworth St

1

S

Queen St

2

3

The Terrace

6

Phillimore St

Short St

Market St

Leake St

William St

PARRY ST

Fairbairn St

Fothergill St

High St

Pakenham St

Bannister St

5

4

Essex Ln

Collie St

Essex St

Norfolk St

South Tce

N

Convicts to Cappuccinos

Fremantle's café society, and the convict heritage

Start

Fremantle Railway Station.
Fremantle train or buses 105,
151, 159 from Perth City Busport.

Finish

Fremantle Museum and Arts
Centre. Fremantle Clipper, Ord
Street to Fremantle Railway
Station, (Sat, Sun and public
holidays, November to March).
Buses 102–104 from corner
James/Queen Victoria streets.

Length/Time

4 km/2.5–3 hours, but add
1.5–2 hours if entering the
prison, and 1 hour if going
through the markets.

Wheelchairs

Good access including
a ramp at the prison.

The British convicts, and their accompanying guards, made a significant difference to the population and appearance of Fremantle. Many convict labour buildings still exist, including Fremantle Prison which remained in use until 1991.

Fremantle had become a rather rough and seedy port city. The 1987 defence of sailing's America's Cup, and a more relaxed attitude to outdoor eating and drinking, have given it a superbly restored heart and a vibrant cosmopolitan environment.

The Cappuccino Strip, with its mass of streetside cafés, intersects with the Convict Trail linking an old landing jetty with the great limestone prison.

Walk key

1. Fremantle Railway Station | 2. St John's Anglican Church | 3. Town Hall | 4. Fremantle Markets | 5. Terraced Cottages | 6. Fremantle Prison | 7. Fremantle Boys' School | 8. Basilica of St Patrick | 9. World of Energy | 10. Fremantle Museum and Arts Centre

Fremantle Railway Station |1| is an attractive and decorative building, opened in 1907. Follow the pedestrian crossing, through the station forecourt and over Phillimore Street, to Market Street. Cross over Market Street to the marble horse trough and drinking fountain, erected by a Londoner in memory of his two sons who died out here. Continue past the trough over some lawn, through the adjacent car park and right along Queen Street. This is part of 'new' Fremantle with its rather bleak shops and supermarkets. Cross over Adelaide Street (named after William IV's Queen) to the palm and fig tree lined King's Square, the centre of Fremantle.

Turn right to a sculpture of a sculptor. Porcelli was an artist who produced many sculptures commemorating Western Australia notables such as Lord John Forrest and C.Y.O'Connor. Here he is portrayed in 'mid-sculpt'. Just beyond is **St John's Anglican Church** |2|, which the National Trust has defined as the 'finest example of ecclesiastical architecture in Western Australia'. The interior (usually open) has a massive jarrah ceiling, some good stained glass windows including one on the left dedicated to early 'pioneering families'. There is also one modern leadlight, attractive but it seems a bit out of place here.

On exiting, turn left past two ecclesiastical benches and across a giant chess board to Fremantle's landmark, the **Town Hall** |3|, with its splendid clock tower decorated with black swans. It was opened on Queen Victoria's Golden Jubilee in 1887, designed

by John Grainger, father of Percy — musician and composer. One of the delights of Fremantle is that the tower has been allowed to continue dominating the town for which it was designed. Sadly, the interior is not open to the public. Stand in front of the tower and look left, towards one of the many old hotels that have been restored to their original elegance. The Fremantle hotels used to be quite rough and ready, but are now mostly attractive, appealing places.

Cross straight over into the leafy High Street Mall, and go through to the traffic lights at Market Street. There are good views of another hotel, the National, which has sadly lost its balconies, and of the length of High Street down to the Round House (see Walk 17).

Turn left along Market Street which runs between two stylish commercial buildings, then curves left at the Newport Hotel to become South Terrace. This is the real start of the Cappuccino Strip, with an almost continuous mass of tables and chairs across both pavements.

The right hand side is generally more popular, being shielded from the afternoon sun. One of the most attractive cafés is the Dome, housed in yet another old hotel building. Nearby Old Papa's is the oldest coffee shop in the strip. This is a great food and tourist area, with numerous arcades leading off to the left.

Carry on to the Sail and Anchor Hotel on the corner of the Henderson Mall. This is another period pub, originally the Freemason's, with high pressed tin ceilings and a wide wooden staircase leading up to the open balconies; a good spot for a quiet break and views over the area. Across Market Street is the banded brick and stucco Fremantle Technical College, and over the mall is **Fremantle Markets |4|**. Their design won a competition way back in 1897, and the markets were restored to their original use in the 1970s. They are still the best known of all the markets (and arguably still the best) operating in Perth.

Continue along South Terrace, past the markets. Across the road, the old stone school building next to the Technical College is now used for maritime studies. Towards the end of the markets is one of its stylish 1897 gates, with a foundation stone laid by Western Australia's first Premier, Sir (later Lord) John Forrest. Just beyond is another of Fremantle's old churches, the village style Scots Church (Presbyterian), with a foundation stone also laid by Forrest. Reflecting Fremantle's multicultural society, this is now also the Chinese Presbyterian Church with Mandarin/English services.

Go to the nearby Parry Street corner, with the multi-storey Fremantle Hospital looming further along Market Street. Look left along Parry Street to the South Fremantle Football Club (Australian Rules). You can see the back of the attractive, domed main stand, and off to the right is the high wall of the prison. The football ground used to be the 'green' and parade ground for the convict establishment.

Opening Times

Fremantle Markets: Fri 9am–9pm, Sat 9am–5pm, Sun and public holidays 10am–5pm.
Fremantle Prison: daily 10am–6pm.
World of Energy (Museum): Mon–Fri 9am–5pm; Sat, Sun, public holidays 1pm–5pm.
Fremantle Museum: Sun–Fri 10.30am–4.30pm, Sat, public holidays 1pm–5pm.
Fremantle Arts Centre: daily 10am–5pm; free courtyard music from November to May, Suns, public holidays 2pm–4pm.

Refreshments

Numerous hotels, cafés and restaurants along the route.

Retrace your steps to Henderson Mall, where the corner by the markets gives a good view of the Sail and Anchor. Turn into the mall, past the other markets gate, to three splendid sets of terrace houses along the right hand side. It is here the Cappuccino Strip becomes the Convict Trail!

When the first convicts arrived at Fremantle in 1850 nothing had been prepared. The first Comptroller General, Captain Edmund Henderson (after whom the mall is named) of the Royal Engineers, rented a warehouse for the prisoners and set to creating a convict establishment. Because the convicts were a British responsibility so was their care, and the British set up the Enrolled Pensioner Guard to function effectively as warders. These were retired soldiers who were encouraged to bring their families and settle here.

Henderson selected a hill (for its healthy air) just out of town for the prison, and **terraced cottages |5|** were built for the guards and their families here, on the approach to the prison. One of them bears the inscription 'V.R. 1851' and all are now used as private residences. Two of the rows of terraces (Nos. 7 to 29) are before the William Street intersection and one (Nos. 31 to 41) after it. Beyond No. 41 is the porticoed 1890 Court House, opposite the ugly 1970s parking station. Beyond that are the Police Station and police housing blocks, half hidden behind a stone wall and peppermint trees.

Turn right here into Queen Street, then, where the street curves away, turn right

Fremantle's Town Hall still dominates the city.

along the laneway just after the car park. The curved corrugated iron structure on your right houses one of Perth's popular music venues, the Fly by Night Musicians' Club.

Cross the next road and go through the car park to the steps straight ahead, at the top of which turn left to the **Fremantle Prison |6|**. The gates are imposing but not forbidding. There's none of that 'abandon hope all ye who enter here', despite the prison being modelled on London's Pentonville. Perhaps it's the stone, or the light, or the position, or a combination, but it's hard now to imagine this as a place of gloom and doom.

The prison occupies 14 acres (5.66 hectares). Cell blocks, workshops, exercise yards, chapels and hospital are totally enclosed by high limestone walls. The original components were all completed in the 1850s using local materials—jarrah timber, and limestone quarried on site—and convict labour. Much is still intact, and the prison remained as Western Australia's maximum security gaol until 1991.

It is now a major attraction, but the interior is not included as part of this walk. Guided tours (at a fee) of the prison go every thirty minutes, taking up to 1.5 hours, and there is a self-guided audio tour of the grounds. You can see through the glass gates to the reception courtyard and the second gates beyond.

A short road, The Terrace, runs across the front of the prison. This pleasant street housed the superintendent, surgeon, magistrate, chaplain and matron. Their houses have now been restored, with manicured gardens out the front.

Go left (facing the prison gate) along here, around the fences of the last three cottages and down the steps to Holdsworth Street, opposite a dental clinic.

Go 30 metres right to a line of lovely terrace cottages with bullnose verandahs, and stone and tuck pointed brick frontages, (Nos. 18 to 30.) A most unusual property, with steps like a gangplank up the bow of a ship, is on the tapered corner. The high prison wall looms just to the side. Come back down Holdsworth Street and turn right across the grass around the dental clinic. Just before the traffic lights look at the magnificent old mansion (No. 160) with superb wooden balconies on the other side of High Street. This was formerly Dalkeith House.

Go left, over the intersection, along High Street. No. 195 was apparently a private house built in the 1860s, and one owner stipulated in his will that the Moreton Bay fig in the grounds should not be removed. It's still there, and even the tiny ugly café can't detract from it.

Cross over to enter Josephson Street. At the corner look down High Street to the nearby Victoria Hall, backed by the unsympathetic bare-walled Myer store, and the Town Hall tower beyond. Go along Josephson Street, ignoring the block of flats, then half left into Point Street. There's an attractive group of four 1890 terrace houses here, with balustrades and iron lace balconies.

Turn right into Adelaide Street along the attractive brick pavement, as far as the **Fremantle Boys' School |7|** opposite. This is another of Fremantle's colonial gems, built in 1855 with imposing chimneys and Dutch style gables. The front central section with its heavy battlement feature seems oddly out of character with the rest, and may have been a later addition. The school is now occupied by the Film and Television Institute (FTI) and a cinema.

Cross over Adelaide Street and pass down the left side of the FTI, towards the enormous brick repository which was the Elders Wool Store. Bales of wool used to be piled up in a whole series of such buildings along here, awaiting export. That time has sadly gone.

Turn right along Cantonment Street, past Clancy's Fish Pub, to the somewhat forbidding Princess May Building. This was a girls' school, and the stonework looks strangely as if it has been painted on. Go right into the gateway just before the intersection and follow the path around the building, before forking left across the side of the FTI again, towards the large stone church opposite.

Cross over to the **Basilica of St Patrick |8|** with its two flying buttresses, and round the left side to the open door behind the rather ugly grotto. The inside is cool and light despite the dark, vaulted wooden ceiling. There is an unusual modern tapestry behind the main altar, and there are three different representations of Mary in the small Lady Chapel to the right. The originals of these are all in Italy (both Fremantle and St Patrick's have strong Italian connections), and two of them are carried in procession down to the Fishing Harbour for the Blessing of the Fleet every November.

Come back outside, to the front of the church, and turn right past the 1916 brick parish house with its original roof dragons. Cross over to the nearby traffic island. There is the Marmion Memorial, and the Proclamation Tree commemorating the achievement of responsible government in 1890. Continue in the same direction,

crossing over to walk along Quarry Street. Just before entering it, there's the **World of Energy |9|** off to the right. This is a museum and education centre, presenting both historic and modern methods of generating energy in Western Australia.

Go along Quarry Street, with its interesting mix of light industrial, commercial and residential uses. There are a few lovely old stone houses left here. Just past No. 35, go half right through the car park, passing to the left of the Leisure Centre (good for a swim on a hot day). At the far end cross busy Ord Street over to the impressively balanced **Fremantle Museum and Arts Centre |10|**, with its Gothic arcade, Dutch gables and rectangular chimneys.

This, the state's first lunatic asylum, was the last major work undertaken (1861 to 1865) in Fremantle by the convict establishment under Captain Henderson. He did so well in Western Australia that he later became Chief Commissioner of London's Metropolitan Police. The asylum was built (using local limestone) initially not for the general public, but for convicts with mental diseases who were being transported with ordinary convicts. It then became a Home for Aged Women, and later the headquarters of the US forces here in the Second World War. It was allowed to become derelict and was only just saved from demolition. The project architect for the subsequent restoration won Western Australia's top architectural award.

Walk up the street to the left of the building, to the main entrance into the plane tree lined Samson Court, often used for community events. It's named after Sir Frederick Samson (see also Walk 17), Fremantle's Lord Mayor for twenty-one years, who was influential in saving the building.

The Arts Centre (free entry) is in the more modern (1880s!) section to the left, and houses craft and book shops, a café, an exhibition centre, and studios for craft courses. To the right, the Fremantle History Museum is more interesting (donation entry) and has excellent permanent exhibitions of Fremantle's History, Post War Immigration. A nineteenth century Governor is reported as calling Fremantle 'a sink of iniquity'. The section entitled 'Within These Walls' portrays the building's use as an asylum. There's even an old padded cell. The walk ends here. Buses are available back the other side of Ord Street, or at Queen Victoria Street.

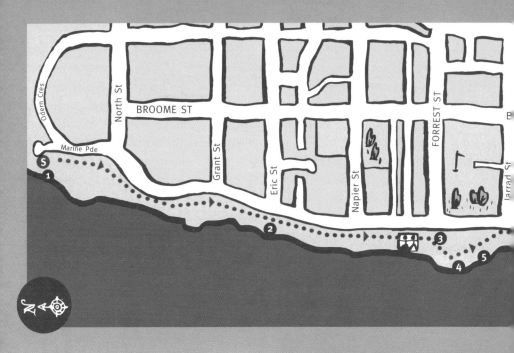

Walk key

1. Swanbourne Nedlands Surf Lifesaving Club | 2. North Cottesloe Surf Lifesaving Club | 3. Indiana Tea Rooms | 4. Groyne | 5. Sundial | 6. Burt's Summer Residence | 7. Le Fanu House | 8. Wearne Community Centre | 9. Vlamingh Memorial

Start

Swanbourne Nedlands Surf Lifesaving Club. Take bus 36, travelling west along St Georges Terrace, to corner North Street/Marine Parade.

Finish

Vlamingh Memorial, Curtin Avenue. Buses: 70–73 Curtin Avenue terminus, returning to central Perth. Trains: Victoria Street Station (Fremantle line).

Length/Time

4.5 km/about 2 hours. Mornings and evenings often give the best conditions.

Wheelchairs

Good access. Return up driveway after visiting Groyne.

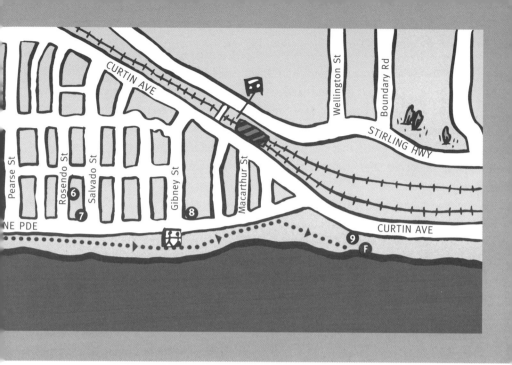

Walk No. 19

Cottesloe–By the Sea
A stroll just above the beaches

Perth has a continuous line of beaches bordering the Indian Ocean.
The summer sea breezes and winter storms sweep in from the sea bringing
a variety of vistas, but the best conditions are often when a morning
easterly flattens the waves and lifts the offshore islands like a mirage.

Cottesloe was one of the earliest beach resorts, and is still a great
favourite – and one of the safest. This pine-studded suburb has some
of its early mansions still surviving among the modern money-is-no-object
edifices. The entire stretch of beach is public land, and well used by
locals for swimming, walking, excercising, sunbathing, cycling and
sailing. The walk follows part of the walking/cycling track which
stretches along the west coast.

The **Swanbourne Nedlands Surf Life-saving Club |1|** is just one example of a grand Australian tradition. Every major beach along Perth's Indian Ocean shoreline has a volunteer group that patrols, supervises, observes and (where necessary) conducts rescues. They mark recommended swimming areas with flags, and try to ensure ongoing safety.

The metropolitan coastline is generally north–south, with long sandy beaches, separated by occasional small rocky headlands. Behind the beaches are lines of low dunes covered with scrub vegetation. The Swan has the only river mouth, and there are occasional offshore reefs.

Proceed south (the sea to your right) along the path by the roadside, above Swanbourne Beach. The beach north beyond the Surf Lifesaving Club has no vehicular access and is recognised as Perth's major nude swimming area. Sadly there's no path in that direction, so the walk goes the other way. Please note that the path is multi-use – you're likely to meet cyclists, families, dogs on leads, and people on rollerblades. Much of the dune area has been damaged by human encroachment, and is now fenced off, with marked paths leading down to the sea. A variety of mostly modern private houses, with unrestricted ocean views, line the other side of Marine Parade. A particularly stylish, curved three-storey house is on the corner of North Street.

The views are over the stretch of water known as Gage Roads, which has a dredged channel leading into Fremantle Harbour and Cockburn Sound. There are usually several freighters anchored there waiting their turn in the harbour. Beyond the Roads can be seen (unless there's rain or haze) Western Australia's favourite holiday location, Rottnest Island (see Walks 21 and 22). Further to the south are Carnac and Garden islands.

The next stretch of beach is a dog beach, and there are packets of 'Poo-ch Pouches' hanging by the rubbish bins, so other people don't step in 'it'.

Go around the curve of a small headland and there ahead is Cottesloe Beach, with its distinctive Norfolk Island pines on one side, and groyne on the other. The cranes of Fremantle Harbour (see Walk 17) loom in the distance. The Cottesloe beachfront proper has a noticeable increase in building size and density, with numerous apartment blocks. One of the delights of Perth beaches is that, with one notable exception, highrise buildings have not been allowed.

The suburb and beach were named after Baron Cottesloe, of Swanbourne and Hardwick, who was a British Cabinet minister. He just happened to be the brother of Captain Charles Fremantle who led the Naval contingent to establish Western Australia.

The pathway splits, with one part staying next to the road. Follow the lower path, past a crossing warning sign—with a speed limit of 8 km/h! This goes the seaward side of the **North Cottesloe Surf Lifesaving Club |2|,** and the well-known eateries of the Blue Duck and the North Cott Café, great spots for a sunset meal. Where the path returns to the roadside, directly opposite is one of Perth's favourite watering holes, the Ocean Beach Hotel, known universally as the OBH. Carry on past the 'Exersite', with wooden exercise equipment and a fitness guide, then a children's playground, before passing left of a covered amphitheatre. Follow the footpath between the Cottesloe car park and the beach.

Grassy terraces lead down to one of Perth's most popular and sheltered beaches. The pylon in the centre of the bay, originally one of a set designed to support a sharkproof net, has been a challenge to young daredevils for many years. The spire broke off in a storm a few years ago, but was replaced – the place just didn't look the same without it.

The beach is edged by towering Norfolk Island pines, which stretch up the hill behind. The plantings were begun by residents in 1905, and are now the town's 'signature'. On the left is the Cottesloe Beach Hotel, built in 1905 and then remodelled in art deco fashion in 1936, and on the beachfront the stylish but rather overpowering **Indiana Tea Rooms |3|**. There was apparently one of the same name here in the early 1900s. It has some interesting touches, and the upstairs restaurant area, overlooking the sea, is light and airy and done in period style.

Return to Marine Parade, to where Forrest Street enters from the left. Originally this was the main street leading down from the railway station and has two lines

Refreshments

Numerous restaurants, cafés and hotels in the first two thirds of the walk, nothing thereafter.

of magnificent pines. A pier, with bandstand, led out into the sea below here and added to the beach's appeal. Apparently on one day some 16,000 people came to Cottesloe by train. The pier was later demolished following storm damage, and the groyne built.

Go down the sloping drive toward the sea, before following the path left along the edge of the beach. On the grassy slopes above is a stone plinth commemorating the landing here of a French exploratory party in 1801. Go past the paddling pool and along the side of the headland to go out along the **groyne |4|**, built in 1960 to control beach erosion. At the end there are good views south to Fremantle, and north over Cottesloe Beach right on up to the tall distant structure of Observation City Hotel at Scarborough. This is Perth's only beach highrise. It seems absurd that the building permit was granted.

Go back along the groyne and path towards the Indiana, but taking the first path and steps up to the right. At the top go right along the path that passes seaward of the Cottesloe Surf Lifesaving

Club (each beach has its own club). The brittle limestone headland is now fenced off for safety reasons.

On the other side of the club take the first path right, down to the gigantic triangular stone **sundial |5|**. The fascinating design is based on the Indian *Samrat Yanta* (Supreme Instrument) built by Jai Singh in Jaipur about 1730. The hours are marked off along the edge of the large, curved metal wings, with the monthly variations indicated by the wavy lines on the surface.

Go through the sundial and up to the single limestone wall. The small courtyard behind the wall has a concentric mosaic (based on a local seashell design) and a dolphin sculpture. This was erected for purely decorative purposes.

Go up to the roadside path and turn right. Across the road is the Seaview Golf Club on prime residential land, and signs warning 'Danger, Low Flying Golf Balls Crossing This Road'. This unnamed section of coast is rather rocky, so there's no swimming.

Go over a small rise to where Rosendo Street goes off to the left past two sad derelict mansions. Their state is the result of conflicts between the owners, who want to demolish them, and the heritage and planning authorities who say they must be preserved. The large double-storey house was **Burt's Summer Residence |6|**. Septimus Burt was Western Australia's first Attorney General after responsible government in 1890, and presumably he had a large family (and a sense of humour—he supposedly called it a cottage). It's instruc-

Tearooms and Norfolk Island pines at Cottesloe Beach.

tive to note Belvidere across the road. This mansion, with an impressive 11-metre high square tower, from the same era, has been looked after and is in beautiful condition.

The right hand derelict can be seen more clearly from the next street, Salvado Street. **Le Fanu House |7|** was built in 1883 and named after an Anglican Archbishop. It has several unusual elements, such as the bay window with conical witch's hat, and a dining room big enough to seat forty people. It is very much a character house.

More pleasantly, off to sea is the small Beach Street Groyne. This stretch of ocean is a favourite for sailboarders, particularly in summer when the sea breeze is blowing hard. They tear along through (and over) the water, leaping the waves and sometimes turning somersaults—board, sail and all. The path here is officially called the Raia Roberts Path, after a Cottesloe councillor who made a significant contribution to its creation, and who died while in office.

At the top of the next rise are the simple units of a hostel on the left. The impressive memorial gates of the **Wearne Community Centre |8|** are on the next corner, Warton Street. At the end of the drive is an unusual seaside structure, with concave (rather than the usual bullnose) corrugated iron draped down from the first floor balconies. This was built originally as the Ministering Children's League Convalescent Home around 1897 (although the date on the wall is 1909). Just before Warton Street is a small plaque next to the path commemorating the spot where the barque *Elizabeth* was wrecked in 1839. The style and quality of the housing is somewhat simpler from this point onwards, leading to two weatherboards near the end of Marine Parade, where it meets Curtin Avenue.

The path follows the coastline, through a lovely little leafy grove and then up a slope to the **Vlamingh Memorial |9|**. Willem de Vlamingh was the Dutch navigator who named Rottnest and the Swan River over three hundred years ago, and whose statue is at Burswood Park (see Walk 10). The memorial is not what it was. There used to be a set of peculiar geometric concrete forms on the knoll, but these were pulled down with a plan to erect something more meaningful. The local council then determined that the site of Vlamingh's landing was uncertain and declined to spend the money. There are now two lonely plinths, one showing the movements of Vlamingh's ships in the nearby waters and up the Swan, and the other giving the bearings of some offshore features. Sorry, Willem.

An artificial reef has recently been constructed just offshore, a short distance towards Fremantle. It can't be seen, but its effect is supposed to create waves when the conditions are right, so that surfers can ride their boards here in perfect safety.

A small grassed hollow just beyond the memorial knoll has a circular drum-like monument to mark the spot where for sixty-five years, a submarine telegraph cable linked Australia to the rest of the world via the Cocos Islands.

The cable station was directly across the road, but is now home to the McCall Centre for emotionally disturbed children. The walk ends here. A bus terminus is 300 metres north along Curtin Avenue, away from Fremantle.

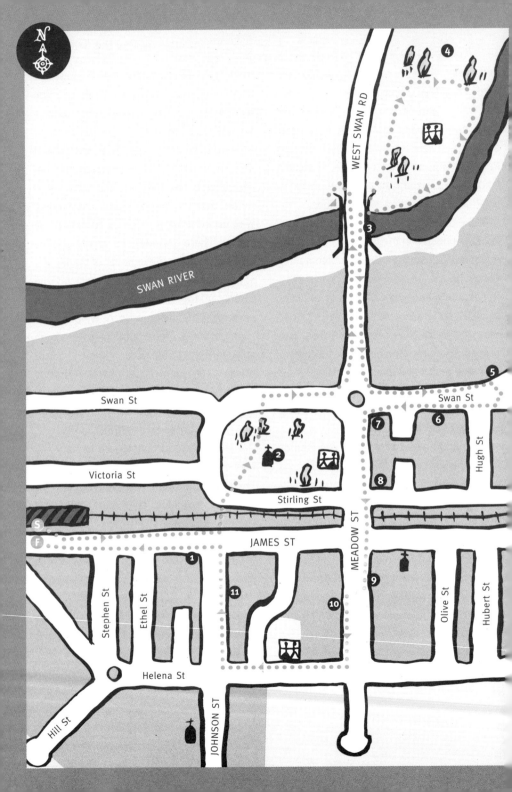

Guildford

Historic village settlement on the upper Swan River

Start/Finish

Guildford Railway Station, James Street. Take the Guildford train (Midland line), or bus 36 travelling east along St Georges Terrace.

Length/Time

5 km/about 3 hours.

Wheelchairs

Uneven surfaces at Stirling Square and Lilac Hill. Several buildings have steps.

Walk key

1. Guildford Hotel | 2. St Matthews Church | 3. Barker's Bridge | 4. Lilac Hill Cricket Ground | 5. Padbury Buildings | 6. Rose and Crown Hotel | 7. Courthouse | 8. Post Office | 9. Garrick Theatre | 10. King's Cottage and Shop | 11. Seaton Ross

Guildford was one of the three earliest European settlements, along with Fremantle and Perth. The Swan was navigable this far, and here were fertile alluvial soils. Guildford was also the first railway terminus.

Agriculture has remained significant, with Guildford the gateway to numerous wineries just across the Swan River in Western Australia's oldest wine producing area.

Otherwise, time and development have passed Guildford by, leaving what's still really a village, with numerous heritage buildings. The entire town centre has been registered on the National Estate, and it's perhaps fitting that many antique and craft shops have opened here. This walk takes in some of the quiet Swan foreshore, as well as many historic buildings.

Outside the station there's a row of grand old trees (sugar gums), many condemned by the local council, apparently because of disease and danger to passing pedestrians, but community protests have resulted in further consideration. A stone plinth, by the entrance, commemorates one hundred years since the railway reached Guildford. A series of shops is across the road, including the rather neglected Apothecaries Hall of 1894.

Turn left to go alongside busy James Street. The Old Village Markets are across the road, and then the **Guildford Hotel |1|** (visited later) all done up in Federation colours. There's a spiral staircase within the pillared verandah that leads up to the unusual corner tower.

Turn left by the traffic lights, taking the pedestrian crossing over the railway lines. Go half right over the road into tree lined Stirling Square, and head towards the church, set quietly in the centre, just like an English church in the middle of the Green. In the original grand design this was Church Square, of twice the size, and there were going to be important government buildings along the southern boundary. The colony hit hard times, and half the square was sold off. The remainder was named after the colony's founder, and later Guildford resident, James Stirling.

St Matthew's Church |2| was built in 1873, replacing one blown down in a storm. The bricks were made from local clay, and laid in Flemish Bond style, like many of Perth's heritage buildings. The church is only open on Sunday mornings. There's a brass plaque here, marking the Swan Valley Heritage Trail, and others will be seen along the walk.

Cross straight over the parkland, where galahs can often be seen (and heard), away from the railway, to the houses on nearby Swan Street. No. 138 is a simple Georgian style double storey house, built in the 1860s. The front is well below pavement level, probably the result of the street being levelled.

No. 132, Riversleigh, is a grand old Gold Rush mansion set within shady gardens. There are enough curves and features, including a splendid wrap-around verandah and a marble column, to make the decorative turret appear just right.

Continue along Swan Street and turn left into Meadow Street (also marked as West Swan Road), opposite Chateau Guildford Liquor Store. Most of the houses are hidden behind brick walls, but No. 27 can be clearly seen. Rose (or Moulton's) Cottage is one of Perth's oldest houses, built in 1842. Moulton ran a warehouse and general store, shipping goods to and from Fremantle. The cottage has been restored, with what are probably the original french windows opening on to the verandah. The shingle roof can still be seen beneath the corrugated iron, while the bricks are laid in an unusual pattern.

Carry on down towards **Barker's Bridge |3|**, and go right at the fork to cross it. The river here is lined with trees and low lying paddocks liable to winter flooding. Houses like Riversleigh were built on the bluffs above the floodplain.

On the other side, follow the path as it curves around to below the bridge. This area became known as Lilac Hill, and a plaque commemorating this is underneath an ancient cape lilac sitting high up on its exposed roots. Go underneath the timber bridge, then fork right through the trees towards the gazebo and brick barbecue. **Lilac Hill Cricket Ground |4|**, just off to the left, is where international cricket teams traditionally play their first tour match in Australia—a one day Festival game. The Swan Valley vineyards start over on the other side of the ground.

Go to the edge of the oval, then right to the river bank. This is very different from the city river (see Walks 8, 10 and 12)— quiet, lined by trees and reeds, and with occasional fishermen, birds and boats.

Turn right along the bank. Just before the bridge there is a view across the river to St Charles Seminary, with its large black water tank. Go back under, then over the bridge, to cross back to the Guildford side. Once over the bridge, turn sharply back to the right, to the small Guildford Town Wharf, a replica built in 1984. This is also known as Moulton's Landing, where the merchant used to land his goods. The river traffic disappeared once the railway was constructed.

Go under the bridge and up the other side, passing St Charles Seminary. The original building was Garden Hill, built for Dr Waylen, the first locally born Colonial Surgeon. Pass in front of an old warehouse

Opening Times

Courthouse (and Old Gaol)
Museum: Sun only 2pm–5pm.
Pottery and Information Centre: Mon–Fri 10am–3pm, other days 9.30am–4pm.
Seaton Ross and Johnson's Cottage: Wednesday to Sat 10am–5pm.

Refreshments

Nothing for the first third of the walk, but thereafter several hotels and cafés.

that is now part of Chateau Guildford. This was built for another local merchant, Samuel Barker, after whom the bridge was named. The loading hoist is still there and the shingles (as with so many Guildford buildings) under the iron roof.

Turn left into Swan Street and go along to the traffic roundabout. The three double-storey **Padbury Buildings** |5| on the left were all built for an early Mayor of Guildford in the late 1860s. They are surprisingly large and in good condition, with vaulted cellars and workshops out the back. The first was his residence and the others part of the general store. There are original timber floorboards, wooden beams, pressed tin ceilings and shop fittings. Upstairs had 'Finer Ladies Clothing' in a large high room, now being converted to a gallery. The paving stones outside came out from the UK as ship's ballast.

The Guildford Hotel.

Go back to beyond the roundabout and cross Swan Street to the grand old **Rose and Crown Hotel** |6|. It has a rather unbalanced appearance, perhaps due to the high pitched roof, which was built to cope with the likelihood of snow! Also, it was built in fits and starts, from 1839 on, and is probably the oldest operating hotel in Western Australia. There are high ceilings, and the extensive cellars have been converted to a bar (open during usual licensing hours). Care needs to be taken with the steep stairs and the low flying beams. In the middle of the cellar is a well, now covered by a metal grille, and in a corner the bricked-off entry to a tunnel. Both were constructed by convicts who arrived in Western Australia in the 1850s. The well water was used for brewing beer, and the tunnel simplified moving goods from the river, though it may also have been to protect travellers from attack. There's a cool, shady garden with a gnarled old plant which is claimed to be the first rosebush in Western Australia, and out the back some 1880s camel stables, which may be converted to an atmospheric function room.

On leaving the hotel turn left along Swan Street as far as the roundabout junction with Meadow Street, which is Guildford's most historic street and part of a specific Conservation Area. The **Courthouse** |7|, with its pitted Flemish Bond brickwork and roof shingles half hidden, is on the corner. Designed by the great colonial architect, Richard Jewell, it was built in 1866 and remained a courthouse for over one hundred years. It's now the main building of the Guildford museum displaying local memorabilia.

Continue past the front of the Courthouse to the stable-like Old Gaol (now also part of the museum) behind the frame for the Curfew Bell. The remaining 1841 structure is set back from the footpath, with brick outlines in the ground showing later (but since demolished) additions. It's interesting to realise that some of Perth's oldest buildings, such as Fremantle's Round House, were its early gaols. Old tools and machinery are displayed at the rear, and Taylor's Cottage is tucked away in the corner of the yard. It's easy to miss, being so dark and tiny. It was moved to be part of the museum from its original site at the other end of Meadow Street—and you wonder that it didn't disintegrate.

Go back to the footpath and left to the next building, which is now a Pottery and Information Centre. There is a private 1898 red post box outside—mail is collected regularly and taken to the Post Office. Next door, looking like a church, is the Mechanics' Institute. This was the first public hall, built in 1865, for the 'moral and intellectual betterment' of the district. It has been a library and a museum and is now home for Oliver's Music Hall, which performs regularly throughout the year. Guildford's distinctive **Post Office |8|**, on the next corner,

was built in 1900 on the site of the old convict depot, and is still in use. It was a reflection of Guildford's importance that, when convicts arrived in Western Australia in 1850, this was one of the first towns to which they were sent.

Over to the right is Stirling Square, surrounded by magnificent old sugar gums, some planted in 1874 to celebrate Guildford becoming a municipality. The Stirling Memorial Gates, sitting all on their own, seem to be looking for a home, and St Matthew's Church can be seen through the trees, beyond the Cenotaph.

Go over the railway line, using the pedestrian crossing, to the traffic lights. Look back at the Post Office for a good perspective, and then across the road to the art deco Council Chambers and Guildford Town Hall. Diagonally opposite is the Stirling Arms, which has made an excellent job of concealing its 1850s origins.

James Street is a fairly busy road, which tends to divide Guildford. Another drawback is that the town is directly beneath the main flight path to the airport. Jumbos at 100 metres are not uncommon.

Cross over James Street and go along Meadow Street, past the Town Hall. At the rear, cross a driveway and go past the front of a simple brick building to the entrance for the **Garrick Theatre |9|**. Built in 1853 as a Commissariat by Lieutenant Du Cane for the convict establishment, it has been home to this community theatre group since 1933, which must be some sort of record. The first house on the left past the Garrick (No. 14) was Du Cane's House. Unfortunately there is little to be seen of the original five rooms, though they still exist, partly because he built the house facing the hills —away from the road.

Cross the road to No. 11, **King's Cottage and Shop |10|**, built in the 1860s for George King, a bootmaker. The property remained in family hands until 1978, and has had few alterations. The overlying corrugated iron has been taken off the verandah shingles, which will probably be renewed. The verandah floor tiles are original, and its walls show reverse tone Flemish Bond brickwork. There is one lone battle-scarred cape lilac on the verge, possibly a survivor from when King planted the entire street. Unfortunately the rear of the property can't be seen, but it has some early stables and a 'grape walk' of old trellised vines going past two outside toilets of different eras.

Carry on down Meadow Street, past a couple of attractive Federation houses on the right, and the Fire Brigade on the left. These are said to be the only Brigade buildings in Western Australia owned by a council, and they are still used by the local volunteer firemen. At the corner, look down the continuation of Meadow Street, which runs into King's Meadow Polo Ground, with the Helena River just beyond. This is a major tributary of the Swan, and has the Mundaring Weir, which supplies the Goldfields Water Scheme (see Walk 23), upstream from here. Turn right here into Helena Street, and go past Spring Reserve, which has Western Australia's oldest and

deepest functioning bore, and a cottage with corrugated iron walls, to the main road, Johnson Street.

Go right along Johnson, past Guildford Signs to two superb adjoining properties at Nos. 32 and 34. These are on the site of a flour mill built by George Johnson in 1855. The first, now Whiteman's Atrium, is known as Johnson's Cottage, and the second, **Seaton Ross |11|**, is a restaurant. Johnson was one of a group of Methodist settlers who arrived in 1830 on the *Tranby*. He built his house next to the mill, and one for his mill manager (now Johnson's Cottage). His son replaced the family home with an ornate brick and tile mansion, which became the Seaton Ross Hospital in 1927. The restaurant now has a visitors' book for people who were patients, or who were born here.

Seaton Ross was then bought by Lew Whiteman, head of the Whiteman Brick Company. He was rich and a great collector of antiques and Australiana, creating a spectacularly decorated and furnished home. Most of the collections were auctioned (for charity) on his death, but some idea of what existed can be gauged from the carpets and drapes, and old photos.

Both houses are worth looking through. Johnson's Cottage has lovely old floor boards and unusual ripple iron ceilings, and now features Australian art and craft. Seaton Ross has so much it is worth arranging a tour (phone 9379 2990 beforehand), and the garden café is a good spot for refreshment. There are bay windows, superb floor tiles by the front door, grand fireplaces, Whiteman's carpets and curtains, his velvet-lined safe, and the fine cellar staircase. Outside is a remnant of the mill wall on the edge of the garden, and the coach house (also 1855) in the corner.

Return to the road, and the real world. Look across the road, to the tall corrugated iron structure behind the Drive Through Bottle Store. This was the fly tower of the Vaudeville Theatre, now home to a smash repair shop. Turn right to the James Street corner for another view of the beautifully (and colourfully) redecorated Guildford Hotel. Cross the street and go inside. In the brown, green and gold interior, note the high ceilings and ceiling roses, the superb old jarrah floorboards, and the unusual pressed tin panelling. It may be possible on weekdays to go upstairs, through the Victorian Room and up the spiral staircase to the open tower. Even if you can't, this is a good spot to have a recuperative drink.

Come back out and continue along James Street towards the station, past the Vaudeville/Smash Repairs frontage. Look inside if it's open—there are remnants of the proscenium arch, and ripple iron wall paneling. Beyond this is a row of single-storey buildings, housing antique, second hand and craft shops, and a café. A short diversion down Ethel Street leads to the Curios Warehouse, with a wonderful collection of fascinating odds and ends—all for sale. The walk ends here. The station is across the road.

INDIAN OCEAN

Pinky Beach

6

5

Lancier Rd

Transit Rd

Raven Rd

THOMSON BAY

Strue Rd

Golf course

Kings Way

Kelly St

Abbot St

Watson Way

VINCENT WAY

4

Aboriginal Cemetery

Somerville Ave

3

1 **S**

7

8

2

Garden Lake

F

Henderson Ave

Coleharch Ave

9

DIGBY DR

Brand Way

10

11

N

Rottnest Walk One

Perth's holiday island

Start

Outside the Visitor Centre at the end of the Main Jetty. Ferries from Barrack Square (on the Swan River) and Fremantle (just across from the Fremantle Railway station). Book ferries, both ways, at weekends and holidays.

Finish

Corner of Digby Drive and Brand Way.

Length/Time

5 km/2.5–3 hours. Hot conditions should be avoided.

Wheelchairs

Uneven terrain around Bathurst Lighthouse. Turn back at the cemetery.

Walk key

1. Visitor Centre | 2. Salt Store | 3. Vincent Way | 4. Boatshed | 5. Bathurst Point | 6. The Basin | 7. Quod | 8. Rottnest Museum | 9. Rottnest Island Cemetery | 10. Vlamingh Memorial | 11. Causeway.

Rottnest, located just a few kilometres offshore from Fremantle, has been WA's favourite holiday resort for almost a hundred years. It's surrounded by sheltering reefs, which ensure safe swimming and snorkelling in glorious protected bays, and it has that wonderful Mediterranean visual impact of light and water.

There are strong historical links. Rottnest was a Native Prison from 1839 until 1902, and has WA's oldest and best preserved heritage building precinct. This walk takes in most of the main settlement and its heritage buildings.

It also includes some of the cliff scenery, the best known beach, the salt lakes, and the Vlamingh Memorial. Rottnest has to be considered a day trip, with a morning ferry over to the island and a late afternoon one back.

The jetty where you landed is in Thomson Bay, named after the first settler on Rottnest. The island was surveyed in 1830 and numerous lots marked out for farming, fishing and salt collection. Few were taken up, and all titles were resumed in 1839 with the establishment of a Native Prison. Rottnest is now publicly owned and accessible to all. There are two main areas of settlement, where self-catering accommodation can be rented from the Rottnest Island Authority. Getting about is restricted to walking and cycling, with a few buses taking visitors around the island or linking the settlements.

The lawn in front of the **Visitor Centre |1|** has anchors retrieved from two of the ships that foundered on the reef-ridden shores of Rottnest. With the sea at your back, go left and up the curved ramp, around the end of the high wall. This imposing structure, originally the seawall, stretches several hundred metres around the bay.

Immediately behind the wall are many of the early historic buildings. They and the wall are largely due to the efforts of Henry Vincent, who was Superintendent of the Rottnest penal colony from 1839 to 1849, and again from 1855 to 1867. With great determination and effort, he organised the prisoners into cutting local limestone for walls, burning shells for lime mortar and plaster, cutting beams and building a wide range of buildings.

Just around the bend of the seawall there's a plain white building. This was originally the **Salt Store |2|**, built by Vincent

in 1856. Large quantities of salt were produced by evaporation from the inland salt lakes until the 1930s.

Turn half right toward the shopping mall, which was the centre for the prison farming activities set up by Vincent. The General Store was originally a hay shed, but now stocks everything that one might need for a stay on Rottnest. The bakery is just beyond the store. Turn right immediately before the mall, back towards the bay, and then left along the tree lined road, called appropriately **Vincent Way |3|** (though street signs are rare). This road runs along the top of the seawall and directly in front of several cottages built by Vincent. These have mostly been renovated, and can be hired as accommodation.

The first building contains Cottages F and G (no, I don't know what happened to A, B, C and D), which was built by Vincent in 1840 as a residence for himself and his family, but then appropriated by Governor Fitzgerald, starting a long tradition of Rottnest as a Summer Residence. The windows were made in Fremantle Gaol, and none ever matched.

The next building (Cottages H and J) was originally a military barracks for the prison warders, and extended later (E). Then comes what's known as the Manager's Cottage, with an enclosed courtyard which Vincent started when the Governor took over his previous residence.

Cottages K1 and K2 have, like the Salt Store, been recently restored (note the she-oak shingles) and brought back to the original white. All the other cottages are still in the supposedly traditional 'Rottnest Yellow', introduced around World War I. This house was built for Francis Armstrong, sent here to 'improve the habits and morals of the prisoners', and to ensure that Vincent was treating them properly. Armstrong didn't last long, and the house became the residence of the first pilot, guiding shipping to moorings off Fremantle (the harbour was only opened up in 1897).

Turn back to descend the steps just before K1 and K2, and turn left to the front of the **Boatshed |4|** (1859), which housed the pilot boats. There are two cells and a sentry box to prevent prisoners stealing the boat and escaping.

Continue along at the foot of the wall, to another building with a boatshed. This was the first one built, in 1846, with boat crew quarters added six years later.

Walk up the ramp back to Vincent Way, and turn right between more modern types of accommodation. On the left are wooden bungalows with enclosed verandahs that date from the 1920s, and on the right villas overlooking the beach) built in the 1970s.

At the T-junction turn right into Raven Road. This road leads toward and round a rocky headland, with good views across Thomson Bay and then over to the mainland. The actual headland is off limits because of the danger of cliff collapse. At the end of the road, continue along the fenced pathway that leads around the next piece of headland. This is **Bathurst Point |5|**, and the small rocky island is Duck Rock (it

Opening Times

Rottnest Island Voluntary Guides run various tours, well worthwhile and mostly free.

Historical Walking Tours (covering some of the same ground as this walk): daily 11.30am and 2.30pm from the Visitor Centre.

Rottnest Museum: daily 11am–4pm.

Lomas Cottage: daily 12 noon–3pm.

Refreshments

Café, tearoom, bakery, hotel and shops within the main settlement area, but nothing beyond. Carrying a bottle of water is recommended.

looks like one in profile). Continue round the Point towards the lighthouse. Both it and the lighthouse keeper's cottage were built in 1900. The lighthouse was automated in the 1930s, since when the cottage has been used to house island staff. It's a superb setting.

Climb up to the lighthouse and look round before coming back down the sealed path, then turning right along the dirt track and on to the continuing road. Go through the avenue of trees, take the second road on the right and then fork right, so that you pass beneath the school to your left. Go past the sports ground and up a slope to the edge of **The Basin |6|**, Rottnest's favourite swimming bay. It's worth resting here a while and enjoying the tranquil setting. If you decide to swim, beware of the shallow reefs.

The shores of Western Australia were first explored and charted by Dutch navigator Willem de Vlamingh in 1697. His first landing was on Rottnest, and a brass plaque has been placed to commemorate this. Vlamingh came across the island's quokkas, thought they were giant rats, and called the place *Rottenest* (rat's nest).

Go back the way you came, but turn right along a sealed, tree lined pathway just before the sports ground. Follow the path through the other camping ground. This leads on to a road that carries on past the nursing and police stations to the main road, lined with spreading Moreton Bay figs.

Take the first road right, Kitson, and go straight up to the wire fence, which marks off the Aboriginal cemetery. It's believed that 370 Aborigines died on Rottnest during its penal days.

Come back to the road and cross the open area to the small white cottage, which has recently been renovated and made into a picture exhibition space. Lomas Cottage was built in 1871 for an old prisoner of 'impaired intellect'. It subsequently became known as Buckingham Palace, after it was used by a warder called Buckingham.

Follow the diagonal concrete path to the large building on your right and enter through the arched gateway. This octagonal building was erected by Vincent in 1864 as the Aboriginal prison, and is now part of

A quokka, Rottnest Island.

the Rottnest Island Lodge, the old cells and other rooms having been converted into guest accommodation. Often referred to as the Quad, its real name is the **Quod |7|**, a colloquial term for prison. The building in the centre was the site of a freshwater well.

Coming out of the Quod, turn right past the main lodge entrance to the simple white Rottnest Chapel. Another Vincent structure, this was built in 1858 and served as school and library as well as chapel. The Governor would read the lesson when in residence. The chapel is open, and still in use, with services every Sunday. Vincent apparently made great use of split bean trusses in the roofs of his buildings, and these can be clearly seen here. No nails were used during its construction. The low verandahed building beyond the chapel was a boys' reformatory between 1880 and 1901, and is now also part of the Lodge. Recycling of buildings on Rottnest is an art form. On the left, across a lawn, is the **Rottnest Museum |8|**, with some interesting displays. Built between 1857 and 1859 (Vincent again) it was a hay store and grain mill. The wider area in the middle was to allow a horse to turn the mill.

Come out of the museum and cross back to the left hand corner of the Lodge. Turn right along Digby Drive, signposted to the West End and Geordie Bay. Garden Golf is on the left, behind a Moreton Bay fig, in the hollow left after Vincent had quarried limestone for some of his buildings.

Go into the **Rottnest Island Cemetery |9|**, dating from the 19th century, where a few remnant graves are scattered across the area. The roughly engraved headstones are of soft Rottnest limestone and so have been badly worn by the weather. The tall gum trees shading the graves in the far corner are introduced tuarts, which were native to Rottnest seven thousand years ago, but then died out.

Come back out and turn hard right, up the path along the side of the cemetery. This sealed track climbs the ridge, then follows it along to the memorial on View Hill before descending the other side. There are numerous signs along the track, identifying various plants and animals. Much of Rottnest was originally woodland, but disastrous fires destroyed large areas.

The three indigenous trees can all be seen along the track. There are sweeping views over Garden Lake on the right, and Government House Lake to the left.

The **Vlamingh Memorial |10|** is within the lookout at the top of the ridge, and has a set of plaques on its sides. The brass disc on top gives the direction and distance of various significant features. Note particularly the bitumen water catchment area to the northwest (Rottnest used to have major fresh water shortages), the various salt lakes, and the causeway carrying the road that leads to the main lighthouse.

The lighthouse is on Wadjemup Hill, the highest point of the island. Although Aborigines did not live on Rottnest they called it Wadjemup (land across the waters) and thought it was a home of spirits.

Continue along the path down the hill back to Digby Drive. Go left, across the intersection, to the near end of the **Causeway |11|**. Lake Herschell is on the right, while Government House Lake (left) can be seven times saltier than sea water, and is Western Australia's deepest permanent natural lake (which doesn't say much for the others). The ruins of the Salt Works can be seen close to the far end of the causeway.

Turn round and return to the settlement along Digby Drive. The corner back at the Lodge is the end of Walk One. The shops, bakery, café and tearoom are all a short distance down toward the beach, which has numerous sheltered spots for a picnic. Come back here for the start of Walk Two.

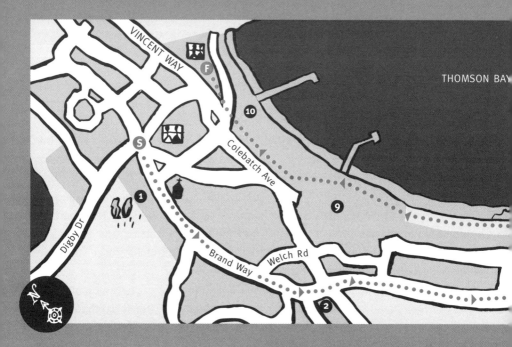

Walk key

1. Picture Hall | 2. Railway Station | 3. Quokka Information Kiosk | 4. Bickley Swamp | 5. Officers' Quarters | 6. Governors' Circle | 7. Clock Tower | 8. Army Jetty | 9. Rottnest Hotel | 10. Dome Café.

Start

Corner of Digby Drive and Brand Way, outside the lodge. Ferry details as for Walk 21. Check the newspapers for departure times. Book ferries both ways beforehand at weekends and holidays.

Finish

By the Dome Café, close to the Visitor Centre.

Length/Time

4 km/1.5–2 hours. Little shelter for much of the walk, so hot conditions should be avoided, morning or mid/late afternoon generally best.

Wheelchairs

Not suitable for wheelchairs.

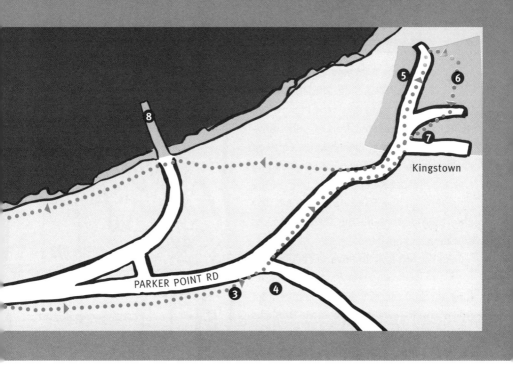

Rottnest Walk Two

Kingstown Barracks, quokkas and the Quokka Arms

Rottnest Island was a major military base during World War II. Kingstown, one kilometre south of the main settlement, was built as a military barracks in the years leading up to the war, and remained as such until 1985. The barracks are now used for a youth hostel, and for school and other groups attending Environmental Awareness Courses.

The walk passes the Quokka Information Area, and the Bickley Swamp Boardwalk on the way to the barracks, while the return journey includes a section along the beach of Thomson Bay, and a visit to the Quokka Arms.

Turn south following the arrows to Kingstown, keeping Garden Golf on the right. Just beyond this is the **Picture Hall** |1|. Built of corrugated iron, it still shows films during school holiday times. Carry on along this road, past the island engineering and maintenance depot, to a fork in the road next to the **Railway Station** |2|. The little train departs for the Oliver Hill Guns and Tunnels from here.

Take the left fork and over a small crossroad, then follow Parker Point Road on its long, straight route, lined with peppermint trees, south towards Kingstown Barracks and the Youth Hostel. At the fork veer right up the slope. The **Quokka Information Kiosk** |3| is down on the other side, on the right. This provides comprehensive details on the quokka, and leads into an enclosed bush area where there is an excellent chance of seeing the small marsupials.

The road then crosses the railway track (the train service to Oliver's Hill), and immediately beyond that (right) is the start of the boardwalk that leads across **Bickley Swamp** |4|. At one time this was a freshwater soak, and features several species of aquatic and semi-aquatic plant life, in beautifully clear water.

Cross back over both the road and railway line and follow the side road into Kingstown. Continue past the barracks and parade ground on the right, and take the left fork next to the old canteen (Peacock Inn). The road goes up a small rise to what were the **officers' quarters** |5|—with the best views! Go to the turning circle at the

The Kingstown clock tower.

end of the road. The views across Thomson Bay and out to Philip Rock are magic. The rock was flattened in the war, because it obstructed a clear view for the gun battery.

A set of steps leads down to the beach. Take the first flight then turn sharp right along a sandy track toward the cluster of houses (NCOs' Quarters) off to the right. Entry through the small gate brings you into **Governors' Circle** |6|, so called because each house is named after a different Governor of Western Australia. Cross to the far right side of the Circle where another path leads up to the larger building on a small knoll. This was originally the hospital, then the Sergeants' Mess. Take the brick path along the right hand side down to the main parade ground, and cross over towards the **Clock Tower |7|**.

There were two main sections of the army here, the Royal Australian Engineers and the Royal Australian Artillery, and their administration buildings flank the square. The main purpose of this establishment was to protect the port of Fremantle, and there were two 9-inch guns installed at Oliver Hill. They are still there and are the main attractions of the tour of that area.

There were also two 6-inch guns installed at Bickley Point just south of here, and one of them is now in front of the clock tower. Unfortunately access to these sites is not safe. The entire complex was built to a surprisingly high standard, with jarrah fittings and copper gutters. The gutters were because of the fresh water shortage, so all rain water was captured and stored. Leave the square through the gates to the right and turn left back towards the settlement. Turn right just past the tennis courts, along a sealed road marked 'No Vehicles', which leads to the **Army Jetty |8|**.

If you don't want to walk back along the beach, take the road away from the jetty and turn right at the fork. Otherwise, take the steps on the far side down to walk along the beach. There is a rocky section (easily traversed) where people have carved their names. Carry on along the beach in front of the cottages, known as 'Nappy Row' because families with small children often stay here—it's quiet, with safe swimming. At the first jetty cross to the concrete path in

Opening Times

Oliver Hill Guns and Tunnel Tours operate in conjunction with the Rottnest Railway. Confirm times and costs with the Visitor Centre (phone 9372 9752).

Refreshments

Kingstown Barracks has water, otherwise there's nothing until the end, with the hotel, tearooms and café. Take some water with you.

front of the hotel. The **Rottnest Hotel |9|**, affectionately known as the Quokka Arms, was originally Government House. This two-storeyed stone house with turrets was completed in 1864 (the balconies were added in 1880), and was used only when the Governor was in residence—all of about six weeks a year. Fishing and shooting were prime activities. A beer on the terrace is almost obligatory.

Carry on past the hotel, and along the 'Peppermint Promenade' towards the main jetty. Planted with peppermint trees, this was the walkway that led to Government House. Part way along, a boardwalk curves out across the sand and round the front of a new tea room. Just beyond is the **Dome Café |10|**, past which the road runs down to the jetty. The walk ends here.

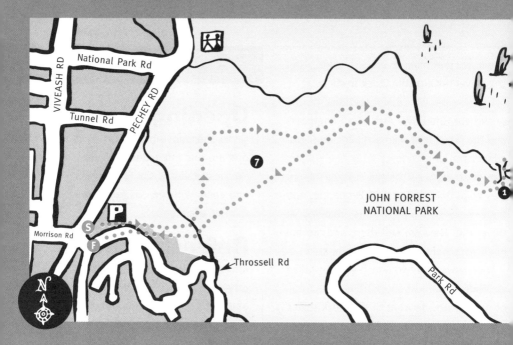

Walk key

1. National Park Falls |
2. Jane Brook Bridge |
3. Main Picnic Area |
4. Deep Creek Bridge |
5. Hovea Falls |
6. Hovea Station |
7. Railway Tunnel

Start/Finish

Car park, Pechey Road, Swan View, by Morrison Road intersection. Bus 323 from Midland Station (train ex Perth), to corner Morrison/Viveash roads.

Length/Time

10.2 km/3.5–4.5 hours. This is a round trip. For a shorter walk you can turn round at Hovea Falls, or even at Park Headquarters.

Tips

Summer is not recommended, unless a cool day i forecast. Spring can be especially good as there w be wildflowers blooming. The track has a constan though not steep, slope. Wear comfortable walkin shoes, a hat and sunscreen lotion. A torch would be useful for going through the tunnel.

Wheelchairs

Uneven terrain makes this walk unsuitable for wheelchairs.

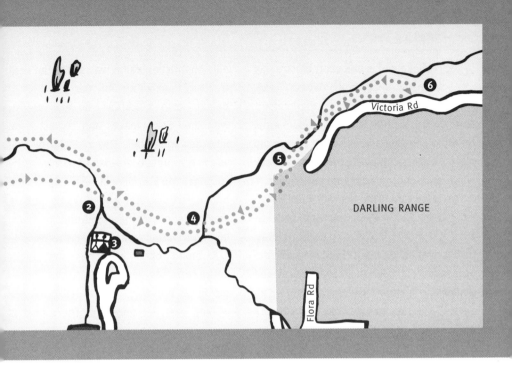

John Forrest Heritage Walk

To the Hills along the old Goldfields Railway track

The Darling Range on Perth's eastern edge offers both scenic vistas and transport difficulties. The Gold Rush of the 1890s created a need for an improved rail link, which was constructed through the Jane Brook valley. This opened up the area for daytrippers, and a National Park was declared in 1900. The park was renamed after John Forrest, the great Western Australia explorer and statesman. This walk follows a trail which has been established along the old railway reserve, and takes in scenic views, waterfalls and historic bits of track, including Western Australia's only mainline railway tunnel.

Pechey Road is one short block along Morrison Road from Viveash Road, with a small car park close to the intersection. On the far side is a white boom gate. Go round the gate and into what was an old railway cutting. Follow the broad gravel track which leads away towards the nearby hills.

This is the start of the Heritage Trail, following the track of the railway built between 1894 and 1896. There was an earlier railway, built further south, but it couldn't handle the necessary traffic for the newly discovered goldfields. Western Australia's great engineer, C. Y. O'Connor (see also Walks No. 17 and 24), had been appointed Acting General Manager of the railways, and selected this route, along Jane Brook, for the new line.

This was in turn closed in 1966, when it was superseded by the standard gauge line through the Avon Valley. The railway tracks have all been removed, but many parts of the trail have leftovers of the original blue metal (granite) ballast.

A sign defining the boundary of the John Forrest National Park is at the start of a high embankment, with sweeping views down to the left. John Forrest (later Lord Forrest) was Premier at the time of Western Australia achieving responsible government, and during the talks which established the Australian Federation. This was also the time when the National Park was declared. It was subsequently named after him.

The Heritage Trail has several points of interest and most of them are signposted along the way. The first is part way along this embankment, to show where the original construction camp was sited. The area is now remarkable for the number of balgas (also blackboys or grass-trees), with their spiky leaves and characteristic long flowering stalk. Beyond this the trail winds up through a series of narrow rocky cuttings. You can almost hear the sounds bouncing back at you—straining, puffing steam engines going uphill and the slow, laboured clackety-clack of the wheels.

A broad open area has the upper entrance to the tunnel back to the right—the lower entrance, which you've already walked past, is concealed. The tunnel is part of the walk on the way back. There are great views into the valley below and, beyond, to the Swan Valley plain.

A white-painted sign on a rock, '1/2', indicated a half mile peg to the train drivers, in a spot where a real peg would have been difficult to place. A variety of birds may be seen along the trail. In addition to the more common kookaburras, ring-necked parrots, cockatoos, galahs and magpies, there is the possibility of sighting a splendid wren. These tiny, brilliant blue birds are quite inquisitive and can sometimes be seen flitting from bush to bush next to the track. The sound of Jane Brook, down in the valley, can usually be heard in winter and spring, especially where it tumbles 17 metres over a massive granite outcrop at **National Park Falls |1|**. A footbridge crosses over just above the falls, and this is also part of the return route.

The trail now winds along close to the river, which is lined by bright green Watsonia lilies, a pest brought in from South Africa. Another footbridge crosses the river, and the trees on either side are bigger and more frequent. The ruins of the old National Park Station, built especially for the day trippers, (including the base of what would have been the waiting room), can be seen. Only 70 metres further on is the **Jane Brook Bridge |2|**, which was originally a 62-metre wooden construction.

There are paths, steps, rock gardens and buildings all visible through the trees to the right, also a small weir, creating a natural swimming pool. The Ranger's Office, toilets, tavern and kiosk are above it. This is the **main picnic area |3|**, which can be reached by paths from either side of the bridge.

Most of the work creating the roads, paths, weir, and all the stonework was done during the 1930s Great Depression, through sustenance schemes. These enabled the workers to keep their families from starvation. Much of the work was because there was originally a plan to create Perth's Botanic Garden here. It was eventually sited in Kings Park (see Walk 7).

After leaving Jane Brook Bridge, keep straight on at the fork (the left side is the Jane Brook Walk Trail). The trail then crosses a high embankment with old timbers embedded in the surface. This was the **Deep Creek Bridge |4|**, the longest timber trestle bridge, at 126 metres, in Western Australia. The structure became unstable but, instead of being dismantled and replaced, it was filled in with gravel, so

Opening Times

Kiosk and tavern: daily 10am until evening.

Refreshments

There is a kiosk and tavern at the main picnic area, two thirds of the way up the trail, but nothing else. Take water with you.

the original bridge is actually buried within the embankment. You can see small quarries either side from where the gravel was obtained. This process also simplified (and reduced the cost of) the task of adding a second railway track.

After a while the area on the left opens up to reveal a broad granite slope, with Jane Brook chuckling over the rocks close to the trail. A footbridge leads to the granite outcrop just above **Hovea Falls |5|**, but be aware of the uneven surface and troops of possessive ants. You may even see an example of the holly-leaved hovea bush, after which the falls were named.

The trail continues to wind uphill, over two pairs of short bridges, as far as **Hovea Station |6|**, the location of which is marked by eight tall, slim, elegant palms. Just beyond the station is a small pleasant picnic area, with a bush toilet (bring your own paper). There are shady trees and rose bushes, reminders from when this was where the stationmaster lived. The picnic fire place is right over the old hearth. This is the turnaround point of the walk, so everything is downhill from here.

Just before the Jane Brook Bridge, opposite park headquarters, there's a track running down the right side of the embankment leading on to the bridge. Follow this down to the stream, where another path joins in from the rock gardens (under the bridge). From here on it becomes a proper gravel path. It makes a change to the old railway track, being less open and providing somewhat more of a wilderness effect.

The railway tunnel.

Next to the stream, it is all set about with shaggy paperbark trees, and occasionally lovely soaring marris and jarrahs. Ignore a track leading off to the right.

Continue straight on where the proper path goes left and over Jane Brook on a small concrete bridge. This next stretch of path is narrower and a bit rough, so take care! It comes out on to the granite rocks next to the National Park Falls.

A rough, steep path leads off to the right, to the lookout at the bottom of the falls. This is worthwhile only if there is a good volume of water going over the falls. Otherwise you might care to dip your toes into one of the cooling rock pools just upstream from the bridge, which takes you back over the stream to the railway trail. Continue down the old railway reserve. There is a small rocky outcrop on the right where the track curves left. This is approximately where a runaway train crashed in 1896. It left the rails at almost 200 km/h, killing one passenger and several horses.

The arched stone entrance to the **railway tunnel |7|** can be seen from a broad open area. If going through the tunnel bothers you, you can follow the alternative route (which you came up) to the right. The tunnel is 340 metres long, but it is straight and you can see light at the other end at all times. It can be walked without a light, but a torch is recommended.

The interior of the tunnel is stone below with brick above. The alcoves were there for workers to retreat into when a train came through. There is only through ventilation, so several train crews suffered from smoke problems when the tunnel was in use (there were only steam trains in the early days). The tunnel is cool and, while the floor is covered with blue metal, it is generally flat and even. It emerges into a narrow, curving cutting, at the end of which you need to follow a rough path to the right which leads back to the main trail. Turn left here. A number of houses appear to both right and left, with splendid views over the Jane Brook valley. The walk finishes back at the car park.

Walk key

1. Hills Forest Activity Centre (HFAC) |
2. Bibbulmun Track |
3. C.Y.O'Connor Memorial |
4. Mundaring Weir |
5. Museum | 6. Mundaring Weir Hotel | 7. Weir Gallery | 8. Fred Jacoby Forest Park

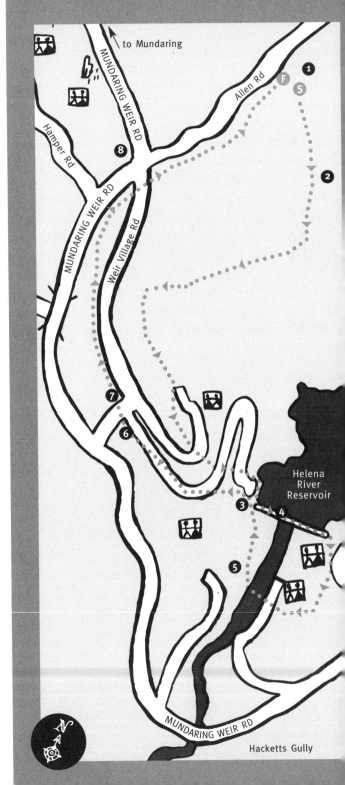

Mundaring Weir

Hills Forest, Bibbulmun Track
and the Goldfields Water Scheme

Start/Finish

Hills Forest Activity Centre (HFAC). Mundaring Weir Road, Mundaring.

Transport

Buses 318 and 320 from Midland (trains from Perth) only as far as the village of Mundaring. This walk is not accessible by public transport. Access is possible by car (several hire firms in Perth), or by taxi from Mundaring. If driving, take the Great Eastern Highway out of Perth as far as Mundaring, then turn right towards Mundaring Weir. After 6.3 km, turn left to the Activity Centre.

Length/Time

6 km/about 3 hours. Summer is not recommended, unless a cool day is forecast. Spring can be good, with wildflowers blooming. This is a hilly region with bush paths and steps. Wear suitable footwear and a hat.

Wheelchairs

Totally unsuitable for wheelchairs.

Mundaring Weir is in the forested Darling Range, 35 kilometres east of Perth. The area has two main claims to fame. It supplies water to the goldfields, and it's traversed by the Bibbulmun Track.

The discovery of gold transformed Western Australia. Unfortunately the discoveries were in semi-desert country, where water was a constant problem. The solution was to build Mundaring Weir, and a pipeline to Kalgoorlie. The Goldfields Water Scheme still operates, and the first pumping station is now a museum. The Bibbulmun Track is a bushwalking trail that stretches 945 kilometres to Albany on the south coast.

This walk follows the track for a short distance, as well as taking in the weir and museum.

The **Hills Forest Activity Centre (HFAC)** |1| is an initiative of Western Australia's Department of Conservation and Land Management (CALM). It encourages and promotes public use of the 80,000 hectares of forest in the Darling Range, known generally as 'the Hills'. Go into the grounds of the Activity Centre. A small rotunda displays information on the local activities, and more can be obtained from the Information building. The Resources building is used for meetings, and the History building will be a museum when funds permit. Note the wildlife motifs in the brackets under the roofs.

The **Bibbulmun Track** |2| runs through this area and over the Mundaring Weir dam wall. The entire track has recently been revamped and redesigned, to provide a greater wilderness experience, to extend it as far as Albany, and to improve the general facilities along the way. The route is marked by small yellow triangular markers, with the long axis indicating the direction of travel. The design on the markers is the Waugyl, the local name for the Aboriginal Rainbow Serpent. There are usually at least five markers per kilometre of track, with more at bends or in areas of possible confusion. You sometimes have to look carefully to find them.

The first Waugyl sign is to the left of the Resources building, pointing past it, and the next is on a tree straight ahead. This is the start of the portion of the Bibbulmun Track which leads to Mundaring Weir. For much of the 2.5 kilometres to the dam

there will also be blue markers, identifying the overlapping Mundaring View Walk. Our walk follows the Bibbulmun Track as far as the O'Connor Memorial immediately above the dam wall.

Most of the forest here has been logged, so this is regrowth and much of it is coppiced – multiple trunks from the one root system. The main trees are jarrah and marri (red gum). Jarrah is *eucalyptus marginata*, so called because the leaves have a fine white line all round their margin. The marri has the large gumnuts (in the tree or on the ground), and it weeps red gum when damaged in some way.

Boxes and long cylinders are suspended in some parts of the forest, in an attempt to attract wildlife back to the area. The boxes are there for birds or possums, while the cylinders are provided for cockatoos (they simulate hollow logs).

The walk meanders through the forest, around granite outcrops and past a wide variety of plant species including the zamia (an early form of palm), several varieties of balga or blackboy, banksias and numerous wildflowers which produce colourful displays from August to October. Balga is a type of grass-tree, with long spiky 'leaves', a tall flower spike, and a black trunk often concealed by a 'modesty fringe' of dead thatch. These plants occur throughout the Perth area, and were a great resource for local Aborigines. There are frequent views of the dam, and occasional bird calls, mostly from parrots and wattle birds. After about 1.5 kilometres the track joins a sloping dirt road with small loose pebbles. Care is needed here. Civilisation appears in the form of forestry cottages. The track goes to the left along a sealed road and round a boom gate, passing behind the houses. The trees here are bigger and older.

Pass through a low wooden barrier on to a real road, with toilets off to the left. Follow the road (and Waugyl trail) over a rise to a small car park and rose garden. Steps behind the roses lead down between shaded garden beds, and across a road. Continue down beneath soaring trees to the lookout and **C.Y.O'Connor Memorial |3|**.

O'Connor is one of the heroes of late 19th century Western Australia. He discarded all the accepted designs for an offshore harbour at Fremantle, and created the river mouth version we have today (see Walk 17). Western Australia's Gold Rush produced another challenge. Thousands of miners and hundreds of mines needed water urgently in the remote semi-desert interior. At times, water changed hands for a shilling a gallon. O'Connor designed the **Mundaring Weir |4|**, and a pipeline (with several pumping stations) to carry water an unheard of 566 kilometres to Kalgoorlie. After a bitter campaign of criticism, he committed suicide before the scheme was completed. A year later, water flowed into Kalgoorlie and he was vindicated. There is considerable information on the scheme, both behind the memorial and in the museum.

Turn left, away from the memorial, down towards the car park, then right just before it, to another lookout close to the dam. At

Opening Times

Hills Forest Activity Centre (HFAC): weekdays 8.30am–4pm.
O'Connor Museum: Mon, Wed–Fri 10.30am–3pm, Sun 12 noon–5pm.
Weir Gallery: Sun and public holidays 11.30am–5pm.

Refreshments

Mundaring Weir Hotel offers drinks and meals. Water is available at the Activity Centre and in the picnic areas around the Weir. Carry water with you, especially in hot weather.

low water, you can see the remains of railway sleepers, left over from the track used to carry building materials to the dam site. Turn right to the dam wall. Take the footpath across the top of the wall, past the attractive, little, lead-roofed intake tower or control room, which is still in use. The tall chimney and adjacent brick building, in the valley below, are part of the original pumping station, now the museum. The current pumping stations are much smaller.

Continue over the wall, with the spillway just beneath. The dam has overflowed only once since the early 1980s, while demand in the goldfields and wheatbelt has of course increased. The scheme has been progressively extended over the years, and now services a region stretching from Dalwallinu in the north and Katanning in the south through to Kalgoorlie and beyond. The statistics are staggering. The network has 8,000 kilometres of pipeline, with an average movement of 90 million litres of water a day. Some of the original pipes are still in use.

The pipeline you can see in the shallows ahead is to allow water to be pumped into the weir from other hills reservoirs. At the end of the wall, go up to the small lookout and another O'Connor memorial. A pathway on the right, just before the road, leads down across a stretch of gravel and past toilets into the wooded area below the wall. Follow the concrete path downwards, then take the footbridge over the river. Go round the chimney then right alongside the brick building to the Museum |5| entrance. The

Intake tower on the wall of Mundaring Weir.

$1.00 entry fee is worth the money. In addition to the history of the weir and the Goldfields Water Scheme, considerable information on O'Connor himself and the development of the goldfields is given. Some of the original equipment is still here, including a Worthington–Simpson High Duty Triple Expansion Duplex Condensing Engine. With a name like that of course it would do the job. Twenty of them were installed at eight locations, and they lifted three million gallons per day from 345 feet above sea level to a maximum height of 1,562 feet ending in Kalgoorlie at 1,375 feet.

On leaving, come back round to and past the tall chimney, toward the dam wall. The red brick operations building on the left has an LCD display which shows the day's volume of water pumped in kilolitres. The small elegant building next to the river was the lower valve house, with two large manually operated wheels to control flow from the dam. 1,040 turns were needed to totally close, or open, the valves—by hand.

Follow the concrete path and steps back up to the top of the wall. Go up the steps in front of you, and half left past the O'Connor Memorial, past some toilets, and along a gravel path. Cross the lawn, veering left, and follow the track up to a sealed road. Go left along this road, with the twin pipeline below you, as far as another boom gate. Walk round this and across the front of the **Mundaring Weir Hotel |6|**, which dates from 1898 when the weir was started. It is still attractive and has modern extensions at the back.

You can go into the bar, then through the door marked 'entrance', and down a few stairs to the passage and the delightful adjoining dining and ball rooms. Half-timbered, with jarrah floors, they lead out to the restored verandah overlooking the coffee shop, pool, amphitheatre and modern accommodation. David Helfgott, on whom the film *Shine* was based, occasionally gives recitals here. Come back out, noting the historic photos, chandeliers and leadlight windows full of different colours and textures. Go out through the brick paved hotel car park, and cross the road to the old brick building opposite. This was the Community Hall (when there was a thriving forestry community here) built in 1908 and now the **Weir Gallery |7|**, featuring local craft work.

Continue past the front of the gallery, and along the dirt track under the powerlines. This is where an old railway line ran, linking the weir to the main track east from Perth. The pipeline appears next to you—you can hear a faint hum if you put your ear to it— and the track has plain orange markers (it's part of the Kattamorda Trail). As you approach a sealed road coming up from the left, the pipeline goes across the valley and past a big pine plantation. The **Fred Jacoby Forest Park |8|**, with picnic sites, is also on the left. Turn right on to the road, and then cross straight over the nearby intersection, on to the driveway back to the activity centre, where the walk ends.

Walk key

1. Gatehouse |
2. Roundhouse |
3. Walk Trail 1 | 4. Walk
Trail 2 | 5. Three Bridges
Daffodil Walk | 6. Grove
of the Unforgotten |
7. Margaret Simons
Memorial Pergola |
8. Concourse

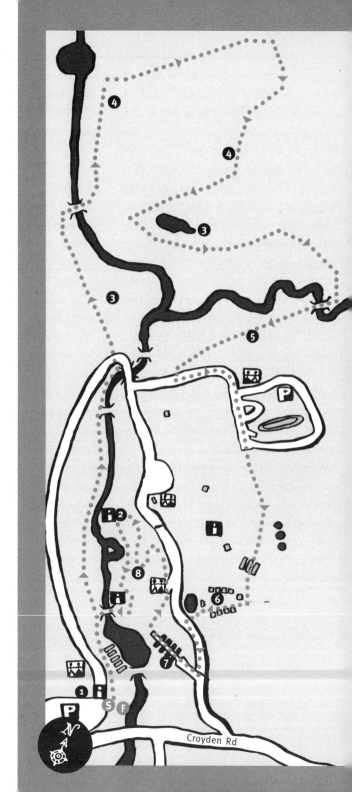

Springtime at Araluen
Tulips and daffodils in a forest

Start/Finish

Araluen Park Gatehouse. Train to Kelmscott (Armadale line), then free Araluen bus leaving at 10am and 11am— only from August 1st to early October (phone: 9496 1171 for confirmation). At other times bus 223 ex Kelmscott to Brookton Highway/Croyden Road stop, but this is 4 km from the park. A free bus leaves for return to Kelmscott Station at 1pm and 2pm.

Length/Time

Gardens about 1 km; Walk Trail 1–1.4 km, Walk Trail 2–1.7 km. Total: 2–3 hours.

Tips

Ideal conditions are any time during spring, but wear good walking shoes if following the trails, and use a stick. Trail 2 has some steep slopes.

Wheelchairs

The concourse is the only suitable part of the walk.

Each spring there's a riot of colour in the flowerbeds and along the stone terraces of Araluen. Within the surrounding jarrah forest, native wildflowers make their unique contribution.

The Araluen Botanic Park is set in a deep shaded valley within the Darling Ranges. Good soils, aspect and rainfall make it ideal for growing bulbs. Each spring some 40,000 tulips and hundreds of thousands of others are in bloom. It's an idyllic setting, with a permanent stream flowing through the grounds. This walk is proposed only during the Spring Festival when a courtesy bus service operates to the park.

Collect maps and other available information at the **Gatehouse** |1| as you enter. Ask for the bushwalking brochure as well as the standard brochure. The maps provided by the Araluen Foundation are generally of a high standard and more than adequate to enable visitors to make their own way round. Most people prefer to just stroll through the garden area admiring the floral displays.

This walk provides a suggested route which follows both bush trails into the forested country above the Gardens proper, then loops back to lead past the major garden features.

Araluen is an Aboriginal word meaning variously 'singing waters', 'running waters' or 'place of lilies'. It was started and developed by members of the Young Australia League (YAL) which sought tolerance and understanding through travel. Changing times and circumstances forced the YAL to sell Araluen in 1985. In 1990 public agitation persuaded the Government to buy the property, and it was then leased to the Araluen Botanic Park Foundation to restore and manage it.

Take the paved path down the slope beyond the gatehouse and fork left past the giant poolside pergola. The path curves through a small area of bush and down to a wooden footbridge. Do not cross the bridge, but carry straight on, keeping to the path alongside the stream.

The path follows the stream, winding uphill with occasional stone steps and views across to the gardens. The water

chuckles around trees and boulders, wending its way across slabs of granite, forming occasional still pools, and tumbling over small cascades. Water adds an extra dimension to any setting. Care is needed on this path, as with the Walk Trails it has uneven, slippery surfaces and trip-worthy roots and rocks.

Go past the Old Dunnies, which look a bit like old stone prison cells. Dunny is the Australian expression for a bush toilet. Further on, the **Roundhouse |2|** (it's actually rectangular) is on the other side of the stream. The path splits and re-joins, and goes past a couple of sets of cascades and another footbridge. Carry on as far as the sealed road, which crosses the stream (on the right) at Bennett Bridge and then heads back towards the gardens.

Turn left along the sealed road for 20 metres and then follow the gravel road off to the right, to follow **Walk Trail 1 |3|**. Go left at the fork and pass through the gate in the high fence ahead. The fence is designed to protect and enclose wildlife including kangaroos and emus. You should pause occasionally along the trails, to simply enjoy being in the bush. Look around at the trees, shrubs and wildflowers, take in the scents of the forest, and listen to the birds and the wind in the leaves.

Each trail is marked by small coloured triangular flashes, to simplify the route, as there are a number of potentially confusing tracks. Trail 1 uses red flashes, while Trail 2 is marked by yellow ones. Wildflowers grow well in jarrah woodland, though a bit later in these cool grounds than elsewhere in Perth—they're generally best here in late September. There's a great variety of species, shapes, styles and colours, with the blue lechenaultia perhaps the most striking. Spider orchids can be seen, often in shady areas, but they require keen eyes.

The trail winds its way through open woodland, with the stream below to the right. After 300 metres take the right fork and continue on until you cross the stream at a small bridge. Fork left on to what is now **Walk Trail 2 |4|** (yellow flashes), while Trail 1 veers back down to the right.

Stay now on this side of the stream as the track winds upwards. Turn sharp right where you enter an open area with a dam off to the left. The dam supplies much of the summertime water for the gardens. This general area (around Araluen) has superb quality water, underground and issuing from several springs. Much of it is used commercially, for fruit orchards such as the one visible up the hill, and also by two of Perth's bottled water suppliers.

This next section of the walk is quite steep and climbs to the highest point of the property, about 100 metres above the gardens. This is the best piece of woodland, with several grand old trees, but much is regrowth. The area had been logged before YAL bought Araluen in 1929, and then shortage of funds caused YAL to bring in the loggers again in the 1950s. Most of the bigger trees are jarrah, once known as Swan Valley Mahogany, though there's also marri (redgum) and blackbutt.

Opening Times

Araluen Botanic Park: daily 9am–6pm. Entry fees apply.

Refreshments

Only at Chalet Healy and refreshment van (springtime only). There are free electric barbecues and numerous picnic tables if you want to bring your own supplies.

Near the top of the slope there's a patch of bull banksia on the right. This produces large yellow cylinders of blossom from October to January.

Turn right at the top of the hill, and descend until the perimeter fence comes to the edge of the track. After a few metres turn right again, following the flashes. The track passes through undulating country before another steep slope leads down to rejoin Trail 1. Turn left here, where in spring-time there are masses of freesias growing wild. The scent is almost palpable. The path passes beneath a granite outcrop which can just be seen through the shrubs and trees. Grass-trees, also known as blackboys or *Xanthorrhoea*, grow in profusion around here. There are a few venerable examples, with tall, twisted, gnarled, black (thus the name) trunks beneath spiky tufted skirts.

The path twists and turns for several hundred metres before passing through another gate in the wildlife fence. Turn right after 15 metres and then go left at the fork. You leave Walk Trail 2 here, to join what's known as the **Three Bridges Daffodil Walk |5|**. The path goes over two of the bridges, close to a large pipe out of which water gushes. A major reservoir is several kilometres up the valley, and part of the compensation for properties downstream was to maintain some water flow. This means that Araluen has flowing streams throughout the year.

One unusual recent experiment here is the attempt to grow karris. These are the gigantic trees that only grow in the state's

Forty thousand tulips bloom during the Spring Festival.

wet southwest, but surprisingly Araluen has similar rainfall and soil to this region, so perhaps these trees will tower over Araluen by about the year 2100. The path leads through a semi-cleared area with numerous varieties of paeonies, some 60,000 daffodils, and several rustic seats.

Go left at the fork up to the sealed road, turn left up the road and follow the curve. Opposite the car park and rose garden (pruned in spring) take the gravel path that leads away from the road. Turn down the path to the right 40 metres before the water tanks. This section of hillside has terraced paths between clumps of granite and towering trees, with cool views over to the opposite slopes.

Follow the path to the stone and timber pergola, and then turn left to the timber viewing platform. Each of the buildings and features within the gardens has a descriptive plaque, with numerous quotes from *The Boomerang* which was the YAL journal. The platform looks down on the **Grove of the Unforgotten |6|**.

YAL was founded in 1909 and five hundred members volunteered for service in the First World War. Eighty-eight died and there are eighty-nine pencil pines planted here, one in memory of each dead soldier plus one for the unknown soldier. The grove is in the shape of a lyre, the symbol of music, with a series of small waterfalls down the centre leading into the Reflection pond. The Australian flag flies here, with beds of tulips beyond. Go down the slope to the pond. Just above it is a giant black-butt standing over a tiled flag, and a plaque in the wall around the pond gives the names of the unforgotten.

Go left on the paved path just below the pond, as far as the start of the **Margaret Simons Memorial Pergola |7|**. YAL was the vision and life work of John Joseph Simons, who in 1929 bought Araluen, which was

meant to be the future home for the League and his 'boys'. That was another time and another way of life, but much of what he started continues, though in different form. Margaret was his mother, and the pergola is a massive stepped affair of tall stone pillars and specially selected jarrah logs, up to 29 feet (8.8 metres) long. Some of the original climbing roses are still there, and long looping lines of wisteria.

The bottom of the pergola leads into the **concourse |8|**, with several paths winding between the beds of massed blooms. This is the heart of Araluen, vibrant with the colours of shrubs, bulbs and annuals especially in spring. There's no point in trying to guide people through these displays. Each person should make their own, leisurely way around the area, looping and doubling back as necessary. It's a pleasure to just stroll around.

At the other end of the concourse there's the Roundhouse shop and information centre on the left next to the stream. Chalet Healy (for meals and teas) is just up the slope on the right.

At the end, go back over the concourse towards the main pool, cross one of the bridges on either side, and walk back up the opposite slope to the Gatehouse, where the walk ends.

Bibliography

Alexander, Fred. *Campus of Crawley Walkabout.* UWA Press, Perth.

Appleby, Richard. *Identifying Australian Architecture.* Angus & Robertson, 1989.

Appleyard, R. & Manford, T. *The beginning: European Discovery and early settlement.* UWA Press, 1979.

Austen, Tom. *The Streets of Old Perth.* St George Books, 1988.

Australian Heritage Commission. *The Heritage of Western Australia.* Macmillan, 1989.

Battye, J. S. (ed). *The Encyclopedia of Western Australia.* Hesperian Press, 1985.

Book of Historic Australian Towns. Reader's Digest, 1982.

Cownie, Stewart & Marie. *Fremantle and Rottnest.* Gallery Publications, 1978.

Elliot, Ian. *Mundaring – a History of the Shire.* Shire of Mundaring, 1983.

Ferguson, R. J. *Rottnest Island, History and Architecture.* UWA Press, 1986.

Fraser, Bryce (ed). *The Macquarie Book of Events.* Macquarie, 1983.

Freeland, J. M. *Architecture in Australia.* Penguin Books, 1972.

Gough, David (ed). *Family Walks in Perth Outdoors.* CALM, Perth, 1996.

Gough, David (ed). *More Family Walks in Perth Outdoors.* CALM, Perth.

Hancock, Denis. *The Westerners.* Text Bay Books, 1979.

Hasluck, Nicholas & Young, Tania. *Collage.* Fremantle Arts Centre, 1987.

Hasluck, Alexandra & Lukis, Mollie. *Victorian and Edwardian Perth from old photographs.* John Ferguson, Sydney, 1977.

Hughes, Robert. *The Fatal Shore.* Pan, 1988.

Hungerford, T. A. G. & Garwood, Roger. *Fremantle.* Fremantle Arts Centre, 1979.

Joynt, S. *South Perth, the Capital's Suburb.* City of South Perth, 1979.

Marchant James, Ruth. *Heritage of Pines, a History of Cottesloe.* Town of Cottesloe, 1992.

Molyneux, Ian (for RAIA). *Looking Around Perth.* Wescolour Press, Perth, 1981.

Oldham, R. & J. *Western Heritage.* Lamb Publications, 1967.

Pitt Morison, Margaret & White, John (eds). *Western Towns and Buildings.* UWA Press, 1979.

Seddon, George & Ravine, David. *A City and its Setting.* Fremantle Arts Centre, 1986.

Seddon, George. *A Sense of Place.* UWA Press, 1972.

Slater, Peter & others. *Slater Field Guide to Australian Birds.* Weldon, 1986.

Spillman, Ken. *Identity Prized, A History of Subiaco.* UWA Press, 1985.

Stannage, C. T. *The People of Perth.* Perth City Council, 1979.

Strickland, Barry & Harper, Peter. *Perth Sketchbook.* UWA Press, 1995.

Vinnicombe, Patricia. *Goonininup.* Western Australian Museum, 1989

Index

Other titles in the series:
Walking Melbourne • Walking Sydney • Walking Brisbane

Notes

Notes